BRUSHED by the SACRED

Lee Beckes

Copyright © 2015 by Lee Beckes

All rights reserved. With the exception of short excerpts for critical reviews, no part of this publication may be reproduced, transmitted, scanned, distributed, stored in any form or by any means, electronic, mechanical, photocopying, recording, or otherwise, without prior written permission from Lee Beckes or his authorized agent.

Please do not participate in or encourage piracy of copyrighted materials which are in violation of the author's rights. Purchase only authorized editions.

Except in the United States of America, this book is sold subject to the condition that it shall not, by way of trade or otherwise, be lent, re-sold, hired out, or otherwise circulated in any form of binding or cover other than that in which it is published and without a similar condition, including this condition being imposed on the subsequent purchaser, without the prior consent of Lee Beckes or his authorized agent.

Published in the United States of America by
Create Space, 2015

ISBN: 978-1518781742

With thanks to my family for their support
and more than cameo appearances
in these pages.
Also gratitude to The Rev. Rebecca Taylor
for her encouragement and kindly editorial
suggestions for improvement.

TABLE OF CONTENTS

INTRODUCTION

1   **PART I: IN PLACE**

5   Section 1:   Along the Way
9   Every day is someone's birthday
10   Another year the gardener digs
11   There was no news today
12   Each year, it seems, it comes earlier
14   Across the valley comes the metallic crack of a bat
15   There are tender mercies
16   It is all and always against the grain
17   Why is it, hearing the best of all impossible promises

19   Section 2:   Finding a Way
23   In a world of war and clatter
24   It is unlikely, we say
25   Molten lava pours into boiling surf
26   There is a mirror in each of us
27   The wind has long since blown
29   Watching the evening news we see
30   Tuesday is every-any-day and I
31   Somehow there has to be a way to move

33   Section 3:   Under Way
37   Keep this prayer as real, Lord
38   There was a time when I thought that summer went on
39   "Catch!," he cried and before I could object
41   Just when you thought it was safe to go back
42   They named him Isaac, which in the Hebrew
43   At nine-plus months

45   Section 4:   Into the Way
49   No one asked me, nor did they you
50   "Remember when?"

52	There are tables where extra leaves are laid
53	I have lived in this skin too long, O Lord
54	Suppose… just for a moment
56	Out of the empty oven of eternity
57	The time is past for metaphor

59	**Section 5:**	**Out of the Way**
63	Tectonic plates grind together until	
64	A shivering tern, wings robbed of flight	
65	Reporters, greedy for a word, grapple each other	
67	White-sheeted hate burns cross-wise	
68	The man in the camouflage fatigues	
70	And still we have not learned	
71	Do this remembering…	

75	**Section 6:**	**The Whole Way**
79	I discover again	
80	I have seen night skies bright red	
82	We are perched tonight	
84	Memorial Day came early this year and this far north	
85	Carefully, carefully, with dental tools and	
86	The dreams of the saints are no less troubled	
87	They move through the house	

89	**Section 7:**	**Away from Home**
91	My mother's great-uncle George stands on the porch	
92	Hands on hips, his Midwestern face	
94	The world has seen far greater evil and closer home	
96	I have followed the pilgrim path to Canterbury	
98	So the past comes to us	
99	Pace off a square	
101	It is nearly ten o'clock	

103	**Section 8:**	**The Way Home**
105	A 747, flaps down, eases into Kennedy International	
106	I wish it was over, she said	
107	We find Thanksgiving sandwiched	
108	Grateful, but not for the grand and usual	

109	A small word, buried in the avalanche
110	The turkey bastes nicely in the oven

111	**Section 9:**	**Way to Go**
113	I never liked the word	
115	The Speaker gazes out from the podium	

117	**PART II: IN TIME**

121	**Section 1:**	**Birth**
125	All births are the same	
126	Between the 'yes' and 'no'	
127	Tiny hooves pick the distance	
128	The house is full of pilgrims	
129	Angels forget how easily joy fills a sky	
130	Christmas is manger and carols	
131	Glory always falls, it seems	
132	Carpenters make unlikely dreamers	
133	On a night you can't sleep	
134	Startled, yet she surrenders the child	
135	They did not *happen* to be there	
136	She was a young woman when the workers	
137	The Magi (from which we get the word magic)	
138	The wise can sometimes be so naïve	
139	Draw a line from Babylon to Jerusalem	
141	The wise men, unwisely, disrupt Bethlehem's peace	
142	There is room enough	
143	Once in awhile	
144	Now we stand at the edge of an age	

145	**Section 2:**	**Death**
149	Out of sight, out of mind	
150	At the age of ninety-five she looked in the mirror	
152	"Ashes to ashes, dust to dust…"	
153	There is more forehead this year than last	
154	In need of a transplant…	
155	Spring is coming, but it is not here… and no one	
156	It would not take me forty days to find my appetite	

157	Still wet from John's washing
159	Who *is* this turner of tables who with whip of cords
160	It takes a thief, they say
161	Every life arcs to a single moment
162	Gnarled and bunioned, blistered, splayed and dirty
164	It was not the best time to step in…
165	But he didn't die, not in the moment
167	Already the body stiffens in the constricting linen
169	**Section 3: Resurrection**
173	Where do you go from there
174	All that is buried, is not raised
175	If they had found what they were looking for
176	In face of all the deaths this dying century
177	Who was that "other" Mary who
178	In that dead stick prose
180	The shroud is cast, the sheet is spread
181	The words fall like stones in a pool
182	There comes a time when heaven
183	So the heaven-sent Son carries back to the Father
184	There are any number of tour guides in Palestine
185	It is the day after Easter and what has changed?
187	**Section 4: Rebirth**
191	The touch of cloth and flesh
192	We would have held him
194	Perhaps it would help
195	suppose the copier broke down and
196	Sounded like…
198	The landscape of our age is littered
199	Choked with mucous, wet from the womb
200	Now the familiar fire returns
201	This is not fast food. It will wait
202	Lord Jesus, one day
203	**EPILOGUE: BEGINNING**
205	In the beginning was the word…

All scripture quotes are from the New Revised Standard Version unless otherwise noted.

INTRODUCTION

The writer of Exodus tells us that when Moses went up the mountain to meet with God, the people stayed below, and when Moses returned, his face shone so brightly that the people could not bear to look at him. The Gospels tell us that Jesus led his three disciples up the mountain where his face shown like the sun and when they heard the voice of God they fell to the ground overcome with fear.

Most of us, like the Israelites in the wilderness and the disciples on the mountain, are not able to gaze directly at the sacred. The following offerings of words are not first accounts of face to face meetings with the holy but are rather glimpses out of the corner of the eye, whispers of the transcendent. To be brushed by the sacred is to feel the hint of wings and the rustling breeze in a stand of pines.

I have come to suspect that the sacred is most mercifully revealed in the ordinary and offers us enough raw presence to startle the soul and race any heart. These various pieces rise out of the everyday and are intended to be as accessible as a child's drawing or a lover's kiss. Accept them in the spirit they are offered and discover perhaps that the sacred is closer than you imagined.

Lee Beckes

PART I: IN PLACE

O God,
your name is more than our naming,
your truth greater than our truths.
No walls built by our hand can hold you,
yet you freely enter the smallest space.
May this place be refuge for troubled hearts
and respite for weary minds.
May the threshold be low enough to welcome faith,
but high enough to turn away
all faction and division.
Strengthen vows exchanged
and promises made within these walls
in the company of witnesses
or in the silence of you alone.
May all the words sung or said here
echo that Word that calls all things into being
and sings life in all that lives.
We pray that Mystery would find a home here
wooing us to a knowledge deeper
than fact or formula.
In times of crisis and confusion
center us here in trust and resolve,
reminding us that we are not alone.
And when we rise to leave,
brushed, perhaps, by the sacred,
may we find a world made more holy
than we first conceived,
more loving than we first imagined.

(Commissioned for the Groundbreaking of the Wick Chapel on
the campus of the
University of Pittsburgh-Bradford on
September 30, 2013)

Along the Way

*O God,
your name is more than our naming,
your truth greater than our truths.
No walls built by our hands can hold you,
yet you freely enter the smallest space.*

Part 1: In Place

Ordinary Time: *Those times in the church year from Epiphany to Ash Wednesday and from Pentecost to Advent. Comprising thirty-four Sundays (out of fifty-three) in the year 2000, most of our time is, according to the liturgical calendar, ordinary.*

Every day is someone's birthday
every day someone dies
      falls in love
      gives in to hate
            runs away from home
            finds the way back
                  strikes it rich
                  goes broke
   gets sick
   gets well
         finds happiness
         feels sorrow
   misses a plane
   arrives on time
            asks a question
            hears an answer

which is to say:
if you're looking for
      the extraordinary
      don't let
            the liturgical calendar
            fool you into thinking
                today is just
                another day

Brushed by the Sacred

Then he told this parable:
"A man had a fig tree planted in his vineyard; and he came looking for fruit on it and found none. So he said to the gardener, 'See here! For three years I have come looking for fruit on this fig tree, and still I find none. Cut it down! Why should it be wasting the soil?' He replied, 'Sir, let it alone for one more year, until I dig around it and put manure on it. If it bears fruit next year, well and good; but if not, you can cut it down.'"

(Luke 13:6-9)

Another year the gardener digs
at the roots of my life,
turning the soil, adding earthy nutrients
without which I would die.
The work is always at the roots –
I know and feel it;
where flesh touches flesh,
must feed and be fed,
pushes against the sod and meets the rain,
opens to the warming sun and curls against the cold.
The gardener digs, calloused hands grip the spade,
sweat beads across his back:
This is the price of my redemption;
the return – a season of my fruitfulness.

Part 1: In Place

On Vacation in Amish Country

There was no news today
        (if there had been we would have heard)
The mother robin fed her naked young
        (all yellow mouth and need)
        in the nest on the porch
        outside our room
And – oh yes! – the sun came up
and we ate granola with honey
        (and whole milk!)
And two horses driven by a singular man
        (in a blue shirt and homemade pants)
        pulled a harrow through the field
        behind the house
There was no news today
        (if there had been we would have heard)

Daylight Savings Time – March 8th

On the third day there was a wedding in Cana of Galilee, and the mother of Jesus was there. Jesus and his disciples had also been invited to the wedding. When the wine gave out, the mother of Jesus said to him, "They have no wine." And Jesus said to her, "Woman, what concern is that to you and to me? My hour has not yet come." His mother said to the servants, "Do whatever he tells you." Now standing there were six stone water jars for the Jewish rites of purification, each holding twenty or thirty gallons. Jesus said to them, "Fill the jars with water." And they filled them up to the brim. He said to them, "Now draw some out, and take it to the chief steward." So they took it. When the steward tasted the water that had become wine, and did not know where it came from (though the servants who had drawn the water knew), the steward called the bridegroom and said to him, "Everyone serves the good wine first, and then the inferior wine after the guests have become drunk. But you have kept the good wine until now." Jesus did this, the first of his signs, in Cana of Galilee, and revealed his glory; and his disciples believed in him.

(John 2:1-11)

Each year, it seems, it comes earlier
and leaves later.
    I am curious… what does it mean to save daylight by
    losing an hour
      somewhere in the middle of the night?
The hour disappears before the sun rises
sixty minutes later than yesterday.

We are tinkering, of course,
with the illusion of saving, gaining –
no real harm done.

Part 1: In Place

But I wonder what hour I am willing to lose:
        the hour one of my children was born?
        the hour we were all together at Thanksgiving?
        the last laughter-filled hour with a friend?

"My hour has not yet come," Jesus said to his mother
        (she demanding that he replenish the wine;
        he resisting the consequences
        of what she could not yet know).

What hour would he be willing to lose? I muse.

Now his hour hallows all our time
saving all our tomorrows.

Summer Prayer

Across the valley comes the metallic crack of a bat,
   then a cheer,
somewhere a mother summons children to supper,
   a basketball drums against the asphalt,
     ice rattles in the cooler.

It is so easy, Lord, as the light lingers
   over the long green hours,
   to disregard the shortening days,
   calling us, again, into the arc of seasons and change.

If we forget you, O Lord, and lose ourselves in play,
   then call us through the evening shadows
   to share the day's adventures.

Give innocence to our tiredness,
and speak to our dreaming –
   hints of half-remembered Eden.

Part 1: In Place

Mercy

There are tender mercies:
    we hear them in lullabies
      and words that comfort
    feel them in hands that touch
      and sighs that sympathize
    see them in beauty that surrounds
      and seasons that rhythmically come and go
but there are sharper mercies too:
    when pride is brought low
      and power is checked
    when riches no longer satisfy
      and a deep hunger roils the soul
    when ancient verities fail
      and new journeys must begin
    when the skin of what was must be shed
      and what is yet to be is
        with fear and trembling
    put on.

Mercy is the death of us
    that leads to
      life.

Brushed by the Sacred

*"I love the recklessness of faith;
first you leap, and then you grow wings."*
- William Sloane Coffin

It is all and always against the grain
of life as we live it:

this business of leaping and wings.
I have crept

once or maybe twice
to the lip of the ledge and

looking down
fumbled for the faintest nub of a wing

and feeling none
retreated.

There is, of course,
that Last Leap we all must take

the one of a lover into the Maker's hands.
But this first leap

contemplated on the lip of the ledge
is not the last

and I have come to suspect that
before it may walk

faith
must fly.

Part 1: In Place

Room Enough

"There are many dwelling-places in my Father's house. If it were not so, I should have told you."
                                                                            (John 14:2)

Why is it, hearing the best of all impossible promises,
we take the measure of the Father's house and
zone it for a chosen few?

Our sad imagining sees only limits,
our words line up like wary sentinels armed with
rolls of flimsy caution tape
barricading heaven's boundaries against
those whose papers are not in order.

If some of your promises, Lord, seem
too generous to be true,
help us to believe them all the same.

And if the truth of them is wilder than
we dare imagine,
then let us live trusting them so that
we may not stand in the way
of your tenacious love but rather
hold open the hope and the door
            for all your homesick children.

Finding a Way

*May this place be refuge for troubled hearts
and respite for weary minds.
May the threshold be
low enough to welcome faith,
but high enough to turn away
all faction and division.*

Part 1: In Place

A Prayer

In a world of war and clatter
fear deceives us, hate divides.
Words rain down a constant chatter,
amid sights of conflict on all sides.

Here in hope your children gather
praying for a better way;
sister, brother, mother, father –
faith displayed in bright array.

Each has heard in sacred voices
calling from a distant past
claiming promise, making choices,
yearning for a peace to last.

Bind us in one holy vision,
just and loving let us be.
Release us from all false division,
by your truth, now set us free.

Slow to speak and quick to listen,
keep us open to your word.
Hold us to your love's commission,
ever hearing, ever heard.

Brushed by the Sacred

"The wolf also shall dwell with the lamb, and the leopard shall lie down with the kid; and the calf and the young lion and the fatling together; and a little child shall lead them."

(Isaiah 11:6)

It is unlikely, we say,
        that lamb and lion would lie down together
        and get up together again
        unless there be a bit of lamb in the lion
        and a lot of lion in the lamb.

These strange, wild images are not taken
        from any nature we know and yet
        we cannot take our eyes from them –
        wolves and leopards and lions
        with lamb and kid and calf
        restraining fang and fear.

I would like to imagine
        that fierceness might be reassigned
        in service of justice,
        that gentleness be refashioned
        into an aspect of courage

so that both the lion and the lamb within us all
        would journey together
        to that starlit matrix where
        the Babe's hand beckons us yet to life.

Part 1: In Place

Labor Pains

"From the beginning till now the entire creation, as we know, has been groaning in one great act of giving birth; and not only creation, but all of us who possess the first-fruits of the Spirit, we too groan inwardly as we wait for our bodies to be set free."
(Romans 8:22-23)

Molten lava pours into boiling surf,
Greenland calves an ice floe
four times larger than Manhattan,
a chorus of peepers follows the rain,
a doe gazes curiously from the fence line,
two fawns in tow.

We are becoming, all of us,
together in the embrace
of a creation straining to be born.

We are neighbors, all of us,
in the womb of the world,
fellow mariners on the salt seawater that
flows in our veins.

This is not a secret knowledge,
information hidden from all but a chosen few…
this is the fact of life
from the Source of Life.

This is no secret,
but somehow it still comes as news to us…
how then, shall we live?

Kosovo Spring

There is a mirror in each of us,
its silver backing pocked and faded,
into which we dare but sidelong glance.

Every spring takes a toll on the face we see,
even as we look away...
the Easter rain has washed the world and
yet there is mud on our feet.

The admixture of the good we intend and
the evil we do
has brought us to another spring,
another death.

Another people – strangers to us –
yet each carrying within
the same mirror, living and dying the same spring
now become the face in the glass.

If we but dare to look deeply
into the stranger's face (which is our own),
another Image – both terror and hope –
gazes back and invites us,
even in this darkened spring,
to become more like
Him.

Part 1: In Place

For Reformation Sunday – October 29th

(In October of 1517, Martin Luther proposed ninety-five theses or arguments that he wished to debate with church leaders of his day. This is recognized as a critical moment in the Protestant Reformation.)

The wind has long since blown
Martin's protest from the church door
in Wittenberg

Who remembers why the dissident monk took
       hammer in hand and nailed his argument
       into the ancient wood?

Four hundred and seventy-eight autumns have passed
       and as many Reformation Sundays

How shall we explain to the children why the wood
       of Wittenberg's doors still bears the nail prints
       and the church remains still splintered?

Shall we tell them of Luther and Leo X?
       Priest versus pope?

Shall we regale them with lectures on indulgences,
   peppering the presentation with Latin equivalents:
       Sola Scriptura, Sola Fide, etc.?

Shall we explain at length why Methodists (United, Free),
Episcopalians, Lutherans, Baptists (American, Southern,
Independent), Presbyterians (USA, PCA, Orthodox), Roman
Catholics, Congregationalists, Greek Orthodox,

Russian Orthodox, Nazarenes, Seventh Day Adventists,
Assemblies of God each go their own way?

Or shall we pray – with Christians everywhere –
    that God
        would nail our differences to the Cross of Christ
            and re-form us all (at great cost and effort)
                into the image of his Son?

Part 1: In Place

Prisoner of War

Watching the evening news we see,
across a hellish horizon backlit by flaring wellheads,
a ghostly ribbon of men shuffling into welcome internment,
exiting the trenches and the maddening perpetual thunder

A wounded soldier kisses his startled captor –
a gesture that threatens to disarm the truest believer
and we are quickly shuttled live to an Allied briefing,
on to Moscow, the Pentagon, and back to Baghdad
where we are told it is raining

There are those who hope that this
is the war that will end
       the world
Others unfurl the new world order
But those who wage the war
   wish only to return to the world they left behind

One soldier will go home with the memory
  of his enemy's lips upon his cheek
A wound of hope that may yet free the rest of us
  to build the peace

September 11th

Tuesday is every-any-day and I,
middling into the week
on my knees – not in prayer –
sorting papers, debris of long neglect

Then news… first trickle… flood follows
as news too big arrives
a drop on the page, then
the wind billowing the curtain of was
into the room of will be
from my knees I look up,
no nearer prayer perhaps
but a world from Tuesday.

Part 1: In Place

"O Lord, give us mercy from Your presence and let a right wisdom order the situation in which we find ourselves."
(from the Muslim book of prayers)

"The ways of wisdom are ways of pleasantness, and all her paths are peace."
(from the Book of Proverbs 3:17)

Somehow there has to be a way to move
        Muslims and Christians
        Arabs and Jews
        Westerners and Asians
        Iraqis and Americans
        Saudis and Iraqis
        Iranians and Irish
        Egyptians and Swedes
        Russians and Turks
        South Africans and South Africans
        You and Me
past the point where we think the world will be
 a lovely place as soon as everyone becomes
like us
   when we really mean like Me –
it's not too late to pray that God,
        in great mercy,
   would take us by the scruff of the neck and show us
    we either learn to get along or else the planet will be
        given back to some worthy amphibian just now
          coming ashore on a beach in New Zealand

Under Way

*Strengthen vows exchanged
and promises made within these walls
in the company of witnesses
or in the silence of you alone.
May all the words sung or said here
echo that Word that calls all things into being
and sings life in all that lives.*

Part 1: In Place

Another Summer Prayer

Keep this prayer as real, Lord,
as a summer morning.
Let some kid catch a big fish.
Let some duffer swing close to par.
Let two friends share a sunset.
Let some dieter enjoy corn with butter
without remorse.
Let the beachside book have a happy ending.
Let the family reunion go smoothly.
Let the potato salad last into leftovers.
Let us be glad for what we have.
Let the economists, politicians, bloggers,
pollsters, texters, and commentators all
give it all a rest.
Let the light dance on the water.
Let the birds in the nest
live to fly south.
Let all things praise you
and for a change
without words.

Brushed by the Sacred

"Take the fig tree as a parable: as soon as its twigs grow supple and its leaves come out, you know that summer is near."
(Mark 13:28)

There was a time when I thought that summer went on
   forever...
When school was out and life could start,
   the yellow bus would never come back and no one
   would expect me to remember the multiplication
   tables or how to diagram a sentence.
Just my bike and baseball glove,
   crickets and fireflies at night and the summer
   slam of screen doors and sometime thunder.
Now that life has started in earnest
   there is a lot less time for chasing baseballs
   and fireflies; the yellow bus has gone and with
   it the forever summer.
Yet the leaves come out, a parable of promise,
   a summer story told in supple green
   and all the more precious for their passing.
I will put away the numbers and wintry lessons
   and listen to the cricket and peeper frog sing
   away the rain.
And know, even as summer passes, and leaves prepare
   to dance their last – a parable of goodbye
   and know that the cricket, the peeper frog and
   I will be joined to Mary's child in a summer
   without end.

Part 1: In Place

Invited

"One of the dinner guests, on hearing this, said to him, 'Blessed is anyone who will eat bread in the kingdom of God!' Then Jesus said to him, 'Someone gave a great dinner and invited many. At the time for the dinner he sent his servant to say to those who had been invited, "Come; for everything is ready now." But they all alike began to make excuses.'"

(Luke 14:15-18)

"Catch!," he cried and before I could object,
   tossed glove and ball at me,
   standing hands on hips, cap brimmed low, as I,
     taking the catcher's crouch, knees cracking,
     prepared for the first of many fastballs

"Don't go just yet," he said and for once I stayed
   and we talked of things that were:
   familiar and hidden, while knowing him a lifetime,
     my lifetime, I knew him now
     as if just met – first, fast friends

"Watch!," she called and came to me
   across the lawn in cartwheels,
   all knees and elbows and blonde hair flying
     to land in a giggling heap at my feet

"Hey, what's up?," he asks when I answer the phone,
   expecting some offer to add one more
   low monthly payment to my VISA account,
     instead hearing welcome chatter of golf scores
     and what happened at work

Brushed by the Sacred

The kingdom is not, I suspect, a place so much
  as an invitation to a feast called life –
…and I will be forever grateful to those generous
  messengers who refused to take no for an answer.

Part 1: In Place

Mid-Life Crisis

"It was light by now and there stood Jesus on the shore, though the disciples did not realize it was him. He called out, 'Have you caught anything friends?' When they said, 'No,' he said, 'Throw the net out to starboard and you'll find something.' So they did, and there were so many fish they could not haul the net in."

(John 21:4-6)

Just when you thought it was safe to go back
   to whatever it was you were doing with your life
      before he came along
  with his way of making you forget
      what you thought was so important
Just when you hoped that he was snugly filed
  under things to do… someday
There he is
  asking how your life is going, when he knows
      your nets are coming up empty
And daring to suggest that you try it his way…
  and what have you to lose?

You tug the net and realize
  that there has come once more
      in the mid-stream of your life
  more hope than you can handle
      with two hands and help beside.

Birth of Laughter

"Sarah conceived and bore Abraham a son in his old age. Abraham named him Isaac."

(Genesis 21:2-3)

They named him Isaac, which in the Hebrew,
means laughter
because Sarah laughed when told that
in their old age
they would have a son.
She laughed until the tears ran down,
she laughed as tears would run beyond remembering

What parent among you, having held
newborn hope in your arms,
   has not known that in the laughter of birth
     there are commingled tears against the unknown?

Tears are counterpoint to laughter,
without them laughter is hollow
They are the solid earth over which laughter's sky
hovers airy and bright

   What parent among you would exchange *anything*
   for the gift of a child's tears against your cheek?

Part 1: In Place

(Grand)Paternity

At nine-plus months
  she could fill a room with her motherhood
    Even in awkwardness sure of her status:
        child-bearer
        first parent of her generation…
But also, just for the record:
        an excellent defender of third base
        an accurate outside shooter
        an aggressive spiker at the net
Her daughter's birth has, of course, displaced all that
        She has changed: more mother than daughter
        her child redefining us all
Her husband wears his change more comfortably:
        strong and knowing
        her hand in his
He has taken his place and, in many ways, mine too…
  yet I am strangely grateful
It's an old story, a nursery rhyme told many times over
  a grandfather's tale of loss and gain
  willingly recited and usually paired with pictures
        thrust upon the unwary
  yet I tell it gladly and offer it as hope and reminder
        in shifting and uncertain times

Into the Way

*We pray that Mystery would find a home here
wooing us to a knowledge deeper
than fact or formula.*

Part 1: In Place

By Water and Word

No one asked me, nor did they you,
as you floated in the womb's water,
to be born

We were not consulted before being thrust,
red and squalling,
into the world
I did not choose the arms that received me,
had no say over gender or color
or the genes that would determine so much
My name was given long before my lips could form it or fingers
etch it in ink
My assent was not required the day
a long since departed preacher
dipped his practiced hands into a stony font
and with water and word pronounced to me
who I was and
to whom I belonged
in life and, yes, in death
For all this, done without either
my agreement or acquiescence,
I am most grateful
And grateful as well,
even to tears,
that my hands and lips,
practiced yet shaking,
directed yet unworthy,
may stir the water and speak the words
of naming and life.

Table Talk

"Remember when?"
Someone prompts during the luncheon
after the funeral
and the stories begin to flow
and the tears and laughter
and all the reconnecting with people
you haven't seen since the last funeral.

The wedding cake is being cut
and the father of the bride,
in his rented tux and too-tight shoes,
turns to the groom's mother
and speaks of the weather
when he really wants to tell her
how much he loves his daughter and
how fast she grew up and
how he wishes he could have been home more.

Halfway through the burger and fries
the teenager with too-dark makeup and nails
peers over her Diet Coke
and mumbles, "Mom, we need to talk."

Two businessmen sit in a quiet booth,
reports and accounts spread out between them,
and at some point wedged into dessert and coffee,
one leans forward and begins,
"I saw my doctor yesterday…"

Part 1: In Place

Sitting at table with his friends for the last time
Jesus offered his final address,
"Little children, I am with you only a little longer.
I give you a new commandment:
love one another just as I have loved you."

Brushed by the Sacred

"For the bread of God is that which comes down from heaven and gives life to the world."

(John 6:33)

There are tables where extra leaves are laid
  in making space for new faces who
  by marriage, or birth, or friendship
      have found their way to an uncommon meal
Odd chairs nestled against matched sets,
  plates and platters heaped in awkward bounty

There are tables that need no stretching,
  musty leaves stacked in the closet
Faces once steadfast are absent,
  seated at memory's board
making this meal not unlike all the rest

How then to give thanks in all the changing seasons?
    How to offer gracious words as bounty and loss
    churn commingled?

Lord, help us form that phrase of blessing
  that turns our gatherings into feasts of hope
  and feeds us with the Living Bread who carries us
  from memory's hunger to that banquet board
  which knows no end

Part 1: In Place

A Prayer for World Communion

"Nobody puts new wine into old wineskins. If he does, the new wine will burst the skins – the wine will be spilled and the skins ruined."
(Luke 5:37)

I have lived in this skin too long, O Lord,
   like old slippers cracked at the sides
   and smoothly worn
I am comfortable and content
   to shuffle through the familiar dusty rooms
   of my life
I fear the ferment, the wine that bubbles and tickles the nose and makes me want to dance
Dance in these old slippers?
What if someone laughs?

Your wine makes me foolish, Lord!
   I forget myself and think that I can shed the skin
   that has kept me safe so far
I worry that your wine will burst my heart
   yet my thirst is the greater
   and I have lived in this skin too long

O Lord, lend me your limberness
   that I may drink the wine that dances life
   and puts new heart in all who put their trust in you!
Amen!

World Communion 1987

"'This is my body,' said Jesus, 'given for you. Do this remembering me.'"

(Luke 22:19)

Suppose… just for a moment
   that by some terrible lapse of memory
   – a table –
   set at enormous expense,
   sat empty.
Every chair empty,
   every place vacant,
a great feast untouched.
The host moving from door to window and back
   watching, searching the dark,
   listening for sounds of feet on the step,
   the expectant laughter of arrival.

Such celebrations are always a risk…
   invitations are sometimes refused or
   worse – cruelly ignored.
I do not trust memory alone
   to bring me to this banquet.
My memory is flawed
   and my feet are prone to plod in other directions.
I cannot imagine why he risks,
   again and again, the invitation: open-handed
     "do this, remembering"

Perhaps it is more than memory, after all
   a deeper hunger of the heart that brings us to table
   as if some vital issue was staked upon our being

Part 1: In Place

 at just this place and just this time
   as if this bread was life and our hunger
     invitation enough to seek it out.
Hope fires the appetite and memory finds the way.

World Communion 1999

"I saw the holy city, the new Jerusalem, descending from God out of Heaven, prepared as a bride dressed in beauty for her husband."
(Revelation 21:2)

Out of the empty oven of eternity
   the Spirit's warm breath bakes a world into being,
   fragrant and filled with all the ingredients to fashion
   a feast of stars bursting with the yeast of life,
   course after course to embellish the
     Supper of the Lamb and his bride
An extended hand holds bread fresh-baked
   while the other clasps close a cup…
     bread to give us strength,
     drink to make us glad

He invites us to himself so that
   where he is we may also be,
   present now in bread and cup…
His words breathe us into life,
   and in the simplicity that is immortality
   calls us along with our neighbors
   to taste the perfect love
   that has joined Jerusalem to her beloved
   in a marriage fashioned in heaven
        and forged on earth

Part 1: In Place

"Do not let it be said of us, dear Lord, 'this is my body, broken by you.'"

(Anonymous)

The time is past for metaphor
and symbol:
   too many bodies have been broken
   too much blood shed
     not to see at this sacred table
     a real Presence not to be denied

Here we cannot turn away
  avert our eyes
  stop our ears
Here we must ask, "Lord, is it I?"
  and know the answer

Hearing the words which both cut and heal
  our false innocence is sculpted away
  making room for a deeper grace
  that we may leave both fed and hungering
    for a better righteousness
    a final feast, eternal,
      to which all are welcome and
      to which we may be
      in some crude, dim way
        a living invitation

Out of the Way

*In times of crisis and confusion
center us here in trust and resolve,
reminding us that we are not alone.*

Part 1: In Place

Haiti

"As Jesus walked along, he saw a man born blind from birth. His disciples asked him, 'Rabbi, who sinned, this man or his parents, that he was born blind?' Jesus answered, 'Neither this man nor his parents sinned, he was born blind that God's works might be revealed in him.'"
(John 9:1-3)

Tectonic plates grind together until
the land buckles – a geological fact of life
that any earth scientist would gladly explain and
any fourth-grader would understand.

A rogue cell rebels and grows wildly
a virus invades
a chromosomal message is garbled in transmission
a clot breaks loose and blocks an artery – unexplainable facts of
life and sometimes death

The *How?* and the *What?* can be laid to rest
The *Why?* – why them? why her? why him? why me? – hangs
like icy mist in the air.

Beware the explainers and the blamers
who speak of the will of God or
suggest that they had it coming.
They do not surround with help.
We stand on shifting ground.
We do not, I would offer,
stand alone.

Brushed by the Sacred

"Why does pouring oil on the sea make it clear and calm? Is it for that the winds slipping the smooth oil, have no force, nor cause any waves?"
— *Plutarch (A.D. 46-120)*

A shivering tern, wings robbed of flight,
   gazes numbly at a leaden sea whose
     sparkling waves once converted
        the light to diamonds

Earth has been betrayed
       once more
  and turned upon herself
  the graphite sea beneath and the silver blue above
    unwillingly brewed into a monstrous calm

Oil rushed upon the water
  but it is not the water that was troubled
    and it will neither blend nor mend

O God,
      by all the names you are called,
  your creatures kneel in blackened sand
  eyes tearing at a smoke-filled sky and
pray that you will
    wash our hearts with a holy water
    soothe our spirits with holier oil and
   for the sake of terns and dolphins and children
     yet unborn
                    forgive.

Part 1: In Place

"He also said to the crowds, 'When you see a cloud rising in the west, you immediately say, "It is going to rain," and so it happens. And when you see the south wind blowing, you say, "There will be scorching heat," and it happens. You hypocrites! You know how to interpret the appearance of earth and sky, but why do you not know how to interpret the present time?'"

(Luke 12:54-56)

Reporters, greedy for a word, grapple each other
   for scraps from the Simpson trial;
Live from LA comes the promise,
   but it seems we hear more of death from that camp
Baseball may strike,
   while in Cuba there are children of the revolution
   who hope to play in the majors
        (Castro, I recall, loved the game… he pitched –
        long ago – what if he had made the big leagues?)
Baseballs are sewn in Haiti, then shipped north…
   the crowded, rickety boats never welcome

The economy improves
   while the stock market declines – the experts,
        predictably, disagree
Congress would like to outlaw crime and go home
   on recess before school starts – the criminals,
        predictably, won't cooperate

While listening to the radio's litany,
   I glimpse a lone maple branch, prematurely red,
   leaning across the road
   leading up the mountain's spine
Each leaf vibrant against the backdrop of green,
   the crimson cluster gaily warning that soon

  the verdant host will join the last chorus of color
        before the white silence
We are fugitives all: OJ in his cell, Fidel on his island, the Senator promising filibuster, the broker at his computer, and I, in the August of my life –
  marking time by red leaves.
Come, Lord Jesus, save us all while there is yet time.

Part 1: In Place

"It is portentous, and a thing of state
That here at midnight, in our little town
A mourning figure walks, and will not rest,
Near the old court-house pacing up and down."
           – Vachel Lindsay, "Abraham Lincoln Walks at Midnight"

White-sheeted hate burns crosswise
   igniting fears bone-deep and weary
   in a people still choosing the darkness within
   over the many-colored promise without

The angry staccato rap drifts like acrid smoke
   from the city whose better angels
   have been turned away
   homeless
   in the midst of mocking plenty

No prairie-lawyer versed in cadences
   of ancient lessons learned in blood and steel
   steps forward to spin the words that may yet
   hold us fast together, making of us a nation
     indivisible

Now in the night, in little town and
   down anonymous city streets,
   we who long to hear the reconciling phrase
   must find the necessary language:
   linking sound to sound until we have learned
   a new speech that scatters midnight like the dawn
   and shows the dark as only colors
     waiting to be named.

Loss of Innocence

(Oklahoma City – April 19th, 1995)

The man in the camouflage fatigues
   his face painted shades of green and brown
   blue eyes startling in their tranquility
   explains that "yes, it's a terrible thing"
     and "no, he doesn't condone it"
        "but…"

It is strange how easily a switch can be tripped
   a trigger pulled
   in response to some wrong
     real or imagined

Rage wears such an ordinary face
   beneath the painted shades of green and brown:
   colors of field and forest,
     earth tones of growth and bounty

The man in the camouflage fatigues
   blue eyes startling in their tranquility
        is afraid
   his face
     pale beneath
     the painted shades of green and brown
     grows paler yet at the threat of faces in other colors:
       black, brown, red, yellow
    which release words in accents he cannot catch and
    so confuse him

Part 1: In Place

He
   or someone like him
   has brought down fire upon us all
and now, O Lord, we all
              wear the face of fear

Brushed by the Sacred

"From all that terror teaches, from lies of tongue and pen,
from all the easy speeches that comfort cruel men,
from sale and profanation of honor and the sword,
from sleep and from damnation, deliver us, good Lord."
— *Gilbert K. Chesterton, 1906*

And still we have not learned:
  that terror begets terror
  despair breeds despair
    that hate has its reasons and
    evil knows no borders

And still we have not learned:
  that the young must bear the burden
  of their elders' choices
    that the heat of anger
    cannot warm the soul

And still we may yet learn:
  that love continues to have its seasons
  peace its cost
    that every life a world and
    every world worth saving

And now we must yet learn:
  that the heart of the matter
  is a matter of the heart and
    only hearts once broken
    can be open to the mending

Part 1: In Place

September 11th, 2002

(On the first anniversary of September 11th)

Do this remembering…
   is what he told disciples with
   dusty fear in their mouths and
   glassy tears in their eyes
remember body broken
   blood shed
remember the darkest of nights
   the deepest grief
Why remember?
              What good is grief recalled?
              Are there not tears enough?

Grief is a lonely beast
   that visits at unwelcome hours
   lying in wait to spring
     sometimes in a laughing crowd or
     when sleep refuses to invade
     where sorrow has staked its hold
Grief never leaves the house
   but pads from room to room
   at home in darkened corners or
   curled like a cat in the afternoon sun

Death comes to all and
   would fold us quietly anonymous into yesterday
   but grief's claws cling and force upon each loss
       a face
       a name
       a memory

Brushed by the Sacred

No sorrow is like any other
   but fits itself into the unrepeatable pattern
   of one life on one heart

And so we remember…
   not to fan the anger
   although the anger is valid
   not to relive the horror
   although the horror flares and scarcely fades…
but to grasp in gratitude what once was and
   to hold in hope what will be

For it is memory that unlocks faith's door
   memory bridging yesterday into tomorrow
   memory shared like broken bread and poured cup
      that makes us one

No sorrow is like any other
   but salty is the taste of every tear and
   who among us has not in these days
      tasted salt?

Who can know how bread
   becomes body or
   wine blood?
Who can know when unnamable courage
   may steel ordinary hearts or
   prayer spill from lips that never uttered before?
Who can remember when our eyes last turned
   to one another and truly saw as they did that day?

Do this remembering…

Part 1: In Place

Do all things remembering
  that the ground you walk upon and

  the air you breathe are made holy
   by the one who made his home among us and
      in whose death all have died and
      in whose life all may live
            world without end.
                    Amen.

The Whole Way

*And when we rise to leave,
brushed, perhaps, by the sacred,
may we find a world made more holy
than we first conceived,
more loving that we first imagined.*

Part 1: In Place

On the Death of a Friend

I discover again
   the uneasy truth that intrudes
   when what was assumed to always be
   is no more

The voice, now silenced,
   speaks with unsettling clarity,
   the absence now a presence
   fixed in the orbit of memory

We trace the silhouette of one life on our lives
   – no two the same –
   a foolish, necessary exercise
   wrought of grief and gratitude
   for what was and was not

Hope comes, it seems, by way of tears and
   will not enter until
   cliché and platitude are washed away and
   the heart is laid bare of false ease

Perhaps the loss of one friend
   may mold me into a better friend
   in some sudden moment or, failing that,
      at least a bit more tolerant
      of the tangle of our lives and
      a bit more careful of the fragile threads
      that hold us together

Brushed by the Sacred

Labor Day 2000

I have seen the night skies bright red
   from rivers of steel tapped from
   bellies of Bessemer furnaces

I have seen men's faces coal-blackened
   as they rise in cages from the womb of earth

I have seen the calloused fingers and
   sun-burned arms of the farmer's wife (mother of ten)
   stacking sweet corn at a roadside stand

I have seen men digging graves and ditches by hand
   turning the air sweetly rank with curse and
   laughter and
   sweat

I have heard the sound of immigrant tongues
   echoing in the summer night and

I have smelled the riches of cabbage boiling,
   bread baking, and
   garlic simmering
   through the screen doors of company houses

I was taught to trace the wonder of words
   by women and men whose parents wandered
   out of the heel of Italy's boot and
   the middle of Europe's thick heart

Part 1: In Place

All who by their labors, praise God, have built
   the world upon which now, in turn,
   I have added my tale of years
   for my children and children's children to tell,
   in time, as chapters of their lives

Brushed by the Sacred

We are perched tonight
   between two seasons
   like the birds which gather
   for their southward journey

The air is still warm
   but cooling
   the trees still green
   but yielding splashes of red and orange

We are between our yesterdays and our tomorrows
   our memories and our hopes

We have seen bright summer days and
   murky storms as well

We recall moments of laughter and
   deep honest joy and
   yes, relive instants of sorrow's blows to the heart

Briefly, we flock together
   fellow travelers on a shared road
   telling our stories of love and loss
   no two tales the same

Tears and laughter well up in the telling and
   both are embraced

We are knitted together – you and I –
   with colors bright and dark
   from the skeins of memories
   sometimes tangled and sometimes true
But the pattern is incomplete

Part 1: In Place

the journey not yet ended

The road goes on to that glad reunion
   where memory and hope are one and
   winter gives way to an eternal spring

Late Frost

Memorial Day came early this year and this far north
    it was certain a frost would follow

Every morning this week pilgrims returned
    to cemeteries to lift the shrouds
    laid over marigolds and geraniums the night before
A few loiter behind, sheets draped over folded arms,
    to visit with neighbors or
    to pinch off the spent blooms

Autumn frost can be cruel, especially when early
    nipping blossoms
    wilting stalks
    mocking the withered remains
    with bright Indian summer

But a late spring frost can be trusted
    to give way to an undeniable summer
    asking only that we bundle our blooming treasures
    for a few nights more and
    all will be well

Sadly, we view death as the early frost:
    untimely and unwelcome
    but I think it is not so…

It is that late frost that is dispelled
    when the shroud is lifted
    surrendering to irrepressible summer

Part 1: In Place

Excavation

"He said to me, 'Mortal, can these bones live?' I answered, 'O Lord God, you know.'"
(Ezekiel 37:3)

Carefully, carefully with dental tools and
fine-haired brushes
the students, under the professor's watchful eye,
scrape away all that is not bone.

Labeled, numbered, each fragment is
boxed and shipped to a distant museum's back room
where with wire and rods it is joined to
others of its kind
reassembled
so that we may, gazing at the skeletal remains,
imagine the creature in life.

Ezekiel stands before the boneyard valley
the archeological dig of a lifetime and
speaks the Word he is told.

Then comes the fearful clatter of
bone to bone.
No careful labeling,
no wire and rod assembly.

This is not museum protocol.
This is the answer to the question,
"Can these bones live?"
That in this shadowed valley
we are fleshed out to rise again.

Brushed by the Sacred

"As for me, Daniel, my spirit was troubled within me, and the visions of my head terrified me."
(Daniel 7:15, from the reading for All Saints' Day)

The dreams of saints are no less troubled
  their fears are no less real
They read the stars with no more assurance and
  mourn their dead with no fewer tears
They are no wiser than the rest
  no braver than the least of us
They fumble through their prayers and
  sing the hymns off-key
They are certain only
  that they are seldom certain and
  when called to speak
  the words come out all wrong
They lose their place and
  they lose their way
  they start over more often than they would like
They don't know all the answers and
  sometimes forget the question
But you know them when you see them and
  you feel it when you're near them
Don't call them saints… it makes them squirm…
  call them by their names and
  call them when you need them
Stay close enough long enough and
  you'll want to be one too.

Part 1: In Place

"The hand of the Lord came upon me, and he brought me out by the spirit of the Lord and set me down in the middle of a valley; it was full of bones. He led me all around them, there were very many lying in the valley, and they were very dry. He said to me, 'Mortal, can these bones live?'"

(Ezekiel 37:1-3)

They move through the house
   they have lived in for years… each with a space,
   carefully fenced by routine and familiarity
They talk as needed, they do not speak as lovers do,
   they do not make plans,
   they do not dream…
They are, shall we say, comfortable
      Can these bones live?

Another factory shuts down,
   another business boarded up… weeds poke through
   the asphalt parking lot, paint begins to peel,
   gates are chained and locked
The out-of-work fill out the necessary papers,
   they do not make plans,
   they do not dream…
They have been, shall we say, downsized.
      Can these bones live?

His face is young but his eyes are old,
   having seen too much… he lives from fix to fix,
   hit to hit… he carries a gun, a thousand dollars…
He wears two-hundred-dollar tennis shoes and
   a gold chain from which hangs a cross…
   he does not make plans,
   he does not dream…

Brushed by the Sacred

He is, shall we say, out of reach [too far gone]
    Can these bones live?

"Only you know, Lord God, and you alone"…
    Lay flesh and breath upon these bones of ours….
   if living is pain… then give us pain
Prove to us there is life before death and
   how to live until we die…
   show us how to make plans,
   teach us how to dream…
And we shall be, shall we say, born again
    And these bones shall live!

Away from Home

Part 1: In Place

Memorial Day 1999

My mother's great-uncle George stands on the porch
   of his white clapboard house
   proudly holding the sword he never used and
   wearing the uniform of a Union soldier

His long white beard does not hide the dancing eyes
   of an old man who lived long enough
   to tell stories of faraway battles
   in the midst of which, at the age of fifteen,
   he carried water to the wounded and
   the soon-to-be-wounded
   yet still a soldier under fire
   who could not fire back
(He lied about his age to be part of the great war
   fought to keep the nation one)

Now he lies below the flag
   held in a tarnished bronze circle with the letters GAR
   that once glinted in the late May sun
   but on that day in 1932 he was contemporary to
   Grant and Sheridan, Sherman and Lincoln and
   all the boys in blue and gray

He was Gettysburg and Bull Run, the Wilderness and
   Fort Sumter, a burning Atlanta and Ford's Theater...
He was part of what made us who we are and
   my mother knew his voice and touched his hand and
   I knew her lullabies and her caresses and
   I remember and reach out my words and my hand,
   God willing, to tomorrow

Brushed by the Sacred

Grosvenor Square

Grosvenor Square, London, adjacent to the American Embassy, has been called the American Square. In it are memorials to American service men and women who served with the British in the Battle of Britain. From the Embassy a statue of Eisenhower overlooks the square.

Hands on hips, his Midwestern face
   showing the effects of the terror he unleashed,
   Ike looks over Grosvenor Square
He is as far from home as a Kansas boy can be
He wears no braids or ribbons,
   no sign of rank,
   he carries no weapons, and
   there is no litany of accomplishment…
   only a name and a date:
   Dwight David Eisenhower, b. 1892 – d. 1969

A young man slumps on a park bench,
   sipping from a can of Fosters,
   a father chases after a wayward toddler,
   a polyglot of voices echo against the stones
They are, most of them, like me…
   as far from the familiar as Ike seems to be
   in his short jacket and regulation khaki

He gave shape to the world that now is…
   would he know that?
   Do we?

Is there still a place in Grosvenor Square
   for unlikely heroes?

Part 1: In Place

And can the Eagle
   wings outspread over the Kansas Colossus
still call forth
    our better angels?

Brushed by the Sacred

In 1692, a small settlement of about 40 members of the MacDonald Clan in Glencoe, a valley in northern Argyll, Scotland, was massacred by members of the Campbell Clan and a contingent of English soldiers who had been quartered and fed in the settlement for nearly ten days.

The world has seen far greater evil and closer home
  Glencoe is, for us, a world away and
  three hundred years,
  a slow day's bloodletting in our time

Our numbers numb us,
  make us amnesiac at millennium's end:
  Stalin's purges, Hitler's final solution,
  Mao's Great Leaps Forward,
  Verdun, Normandy, My Lai, Wounded Knee,
  Kosovo, Cambodia's killing fields, Oklahoma City
  a century's steady hemorrhage of anonymous death

At Glencoe, the numbers are manageable:
  thirty-eight, perhaps forty-five,
  men, women, children,
  slashed, shot, bayonetted
  all in a morning's work for hardened soldiers and
  bitter men under orders, under orders
It is not, nor ever was, the numbers
  but the magnitude of such and each betrayal

Ten days of hospitality…
    cup and meal shared…
  the iron rule of the highlands, old as Abraham:
      Welcome the visitor who comes in peace and
        do not betray the Host.

Part 1: In Place

Forget this irreducible human transaction and
   our humanity is forfeit

Come to Glencoe and hear
   the keening wind carry a child's cry,
   a mother's moan
Do not come to remember some ancient wrong
   or to fan clannish wrath

Come and consider the fragile shackles upon
   the beast within us all
Hear the rain splash against the rocks of Glencoe,
   see the distant waters pour
   from the veins of misted hillsides

Come to Glencoe
   not as Scot or English,
   MacDonald, Stewart, or Campbell and
most of all, not as a stranger, but a guest
   respecting the dictates of ancient hospitality
   by which we may yet mend
   the dying century

Brushed by the Sacred

Tourist Eyes

"But take it not, I pray you, I disdain,
This is the point, to speak short and plain,
That each of you, to shorten our way,
On this journey shall two tales say."

(Canterbury Tales, The Prologue)

I have followed the pilgrim path to Canterbury...
   a day trip on a crowded bus full of Americans
   with stops at Leeds Castle on the way and
   Dover on the return...

We saw it all
   with pictures, the tourist's awards, as proof

But what did we see?
   Stone and glass and chalky cliffs and
   France fogged out across the Channel

Our guide apologized and assured us it was there...
   we took him at his word

No one told any stories to shorten the way
   except our guide who admitted to snitching,
     as a child,
   apples from the Leeds Estate and
   who then recited snippets of Chaucer learned,
     as a child,
   for ambiance

I cannot prove that I witnessed where Becket died –
   photographs were forbidden – and

Part 1: In Place

I cannot prove that where I stood was the place…
  but this I know: my tourist eyes did burn
  for what I learned had happened and
     I lit a candle to ease the smart

Brushed by the Sacred

Broken Images/Durham Cathedral

In the ancient cathedral of Durham there is a large stained glass window on the western side in what is called the Galilean's Chapel which has been reconstructed from glass from windows broken by Cromwell's soldiers. The light shines directly on the tomb of the Venerable Bede (673-735), historian, teacher, theologian.

So the past comes to us
  Picasso-like…
    fragmented, distorted
     a Guernica patchwork of images
    casting the light
  upon the tomb of Venerable Bede and
  the altars of the Galilean's Chapel
    for each generation to reconstruct
     by its own lights
and yet, by God's grace,
  to make some sense

Puzzling out our race's yesterdays and
  laying them,
    broken and bright,
  upon the altar of their generation's hope

Part 1: In Place

There are many churches throughout the Highlands of Scotland that have been long abandoned due to the terrible population shifts caused by the clearances which occurred in the years after the defeat of Prince Charles, the last Stuart claimant to the throne. Farms were cleared of their inhabitants to provide pasture for sheep and many people were pushed off the land.

Pace off a square
   of rare level heath
Gather stones, laying each
   upon its once scattered neighbor
Truss the roof with beams
   all the more precious
   in a land bereft of trees
Slate the rooftop and
   fence a little plot to bury the dead

Call it Kirk and pray it to be sacred ground
   to keep at bay the devils and the dark
   rolling down the gloomy mountains and
   across the uneasy sea

Huddle around the light of sacred page
   holding to promises made in thunder and fire
   to ancient peoples,
      clansmen like you,
   pledged to bearded lairds
   tied to covenant and law
   who buried their dead in cave and field and
   carried their tabernacle
   into a strange, unyielding land

Brushed by the Sacred

A people who knew invasion and exile
  betrayal and failure
  yet held to and were held by
  the God who chose them

Part 1: In Place

The Kirk at Dunvegan, Isle of Skye

It is nearly ten o'clock
    a dog-collared parson, coattails flapping,
    rushes to the door
    while the faithful wave him through

No stranger could hide here and
      we are welcomed.
      "Sit where ye like,"
      we are told with a smile and a wave and
      we do, finding a place
        close to the front, of course

A kilted man advances the lectern
      while the parson climbs the stairs
      to a high pulpit and
      closes the door behind him.

There is no bulletin,
      announcements are made by the kilted beadle
      who is occasionally corrected
      by the better-informed in the congregation.

The hymnbook holds words alone and
      the Psalms are set to rhyme
      but the tunes are easy, known.

The preacher is retired
      pressed back into service
      his prayers are long

Brushed by the Sacred

The sermon rambles freely
      over familiar ground.

But his words are generous and warm and
      he speaks graciously
         of those whose faith has touched him…
         not all of them Presbyterian.

Then the inevitable offering and
      final hymn… six verses.
Some four thousand miles away
      from those we know and love
      we were, for an hour,
         home.

The Way Home

Part 1: In Place

Points of Entry – Independence Day 1995

A 747, flaps down, eases into Kennedy International,
  belly full of dialects and color
    she takes her berth and relinquishes her cargo
    into the gathering stream of turbans and saris,
      sidelocks and dreadlocks,
      brogues, gutturals, sweet sing-song, and
      the babble of children,
  hands holding passport, visa, green card, and
  yes – still… hope

Floodlights bathe the border crossing
  unfriendly beacons for those who would penetrate
  the porous underside of a nation uncertain of its
  immigrant station
  yet on they come wearing Nikes, Adidas, Reeboks
    running, always running,
  hands empty of passport, visa, green card, but
  clutching still… hope

No shadows dance in the glare of delivery room lights
  the newborn kicks free, blinks, lets out a squall
  having broken through the membrane separating
  one world from another
    her purpled hand seizes the nurse's finger
  she holds no passport, visa, green card, but
  still, still… hope

So the nation, unwittingly transfused once more,
  may yet find again, this day,
her life

The Ballot Cast

I wish it was over, she said,
meaning the harsh words,
the endless plumping and promising,
the dismissal of context and simple sense

Two things I will not discuss with you –
      religion and politics –
as if they could only divide and separate us
from each other

And that is sad, for these are the two things
that might bring us together…
the one in awe and mystery
the other in passion and common purpose

This November I will cast my ballot
for your well-being and trust you
to do the same

Then, when all the ballots are cast and counted,
we may speak at length
of shaping better days and
join our hearts in prayer

Part 1: In Place

Looking for Thanksgiving

Halloween has become the second biggest holiday in terms of consumer spending. Sales of candy, costumes and decorations will total $3.3 billion, up 5.4 percent over last year, according to the NRF study.

We find Thanksgiving sandwiched
between the two holidays
  our gratitude lies cold as leftover turkey
  as we move on to the Black Friday
  of retail hope

Are children's classrooms still adorned
  with the silhouetted pilgrims and
  the brightly-colored birds traced around a tiny hand?
Do we still tell the story of trusting natives
  bringing corn to the shared feast?
        No?

Here is the danger of believing it never happened:
    if it didn't happen, it cannot happen.

Such stories belie our best hopes and
  the truth of them may yet to be.

Be grateful and perhaps discover
  that gratitude may lead to grace and
  all may yet come to table.

Thanksgiving

Grateful, but not for the grand and usual
   items that are brought out for the holiday and
   then put aside
but grateful, all the same,
   for the way the sunlight slants on a golden maple,
   the way leaves crackle underfoot

Yes, I know what the headlines are blaring, and,
   no, I'm not sure where all this is going, or
   even this string of words, for that matter,
but there must have been a reason
I got up this morning, and a reason
   you are reading this and wondering too, perhaps,
   where it's going…
and I imagine a curious God,
   greeting a curious creation
   with a "good morning" and
   the question, "What shall we do today?"
Then stretches arms,
   claps hands together, and
   answers the question with the declaration:
      "I know, let's do something new!"
And suddenly it's Christmas morning,
   the first day of fishing season,
   the last day of school, and
   for reasons I should not have to explain,
         I am grateful

Part 1: In Place

Thanks

A small word, buried in the avalanche of
words that assail us daily
too often goes unheard.
Grazie in Italian
Gracias in Spanish
from the Latin *gratia*
which gives us *grace* and *gracious* and,
of course, *gratitude*

But when eyes meet as the word is offered
a bridge is built over which
two may go together or
when the word arrives nestled
in an envelope handwritten
a heart is lifted.

Such a small word to have a day of its own
by decree no less!
This amazing word,
this gracious word,
can turn any day to the light and
make the most common exchange
    a sort of prayer.

Brushed by the Sacred

"That is why I say to you, don't worry about living, wondering what you are going to eat and drink, or what you are going to wear. Surely life is more important than food, and the body more important than the clothes you wear."

(Matthew 6:25)

The turkey bastes nicely in the oven,
   potatoes boil on the stove,
   pies arrive with guests,
   the annual can of cranberry sauce is opened.

We don't wonder about what we are to eat and drink,
   nor do we worry (unduly)
   what we shall wear.

It is the deeper worries:
   for our children, our families, our friends,
   our neighborhood, our nation…
        perhaps with some imagination, for our world…
   that bubble up in the grace we mumble over the meal
   or later when the house is dark…
     worries nameless by their nature,
   or by our choice (or both)

Then, O Lord, take our tangled yearnings,
   slip-knotted with worry, and
   knit them into a net of hope that gathers
     children, families, friends, neighborhood,
      nation, world
   into the abundance of your Kingdom
   in which panic turns into prayer and
   prayer into living deeds of love and
   truest thanksgiving.

Way to Go

Part 1: In Place

Church Discipline

I never like the word
   discipline
  it reeks of punishment,
  heavy-handed correction
often directed toward wayward children and
  other criminal types

It also seems to suggest
  hefty lifting and sweaty repetition
When linked with church
  it becomes even more dreary
    thin-lipped humorless types
  expressing righteous disapproval

It gives off the stale smell of
      have to
      ought to
      should and must
I confess to not being drawn to it.

Except when I find that when
  by practice and habit
     (two more less-than-cheery terms)
  there comes a certain confidence
  even growth
  dare I say it: strength?

Then I discover that hidden in *discipline*
  one may find *disciple* – student, follower, learner and
so I may just sign up for the course

which looks interesting, exciting, even life-changing,
starting in September with no prerequisites
other than an open heart.

Part 1: In Place

Commencement

The Speaker gazes out from the podium
on the assembled crowd of parents, teachers, and
soon-to-be alums who will commence
in a few moments to march into the same
baffling mystery that their parents, teachers, and
the Speaker are still puzzling out
It would be oh so refreshing to hear the Speaker
clear his throat and say something such as,
"It has been forty-five years since I sat where you sit
and I still don't know what I'll be when I grow up.
The world is messy and nothing will turn out
just as you planned.
There aren't two sides to every issue, there are at least
seven or eight and that's a conservative estimate.
Today's answers will be tomorrow's questions.
You won't save the world but
you may be able to help pick up some of the pieces.
Always keep a roll of duct tape handy.
Don't stop trusting people, but brace yourself for
disappointments.
Sometimes, you will be that disappointment.
Words can hurt worse than sticks and stones
so be careful how you use them.
Never try to explain a joke. Let it go.
You *can* be too rich and too thin.
The Devil is in the details. So is God.
Your cap and gown are rented,
return them in the same condition you got them.
You won't remember anything I just said.
Thanks for your attention. Good night."

PART II: IN TIME

Do not seek the Holy
 as something added on
 appended to a life otherwise complete
See Moses barefoot before a burning bush
 Abraham moving out at ninety and
 Sarah with child..
See Isaiah as the temple pillars shake
 a hot coal sizzling on his lips
  Noah bobbing in the storm
  Jonah in the whale's belly
See Paul flattened on the Damascus road
 Lazarus shuffling toward the light
See Jesus on a government-issue cross...
See the empty tomb…
Do not seek the Holy
 The Holy will find you
And when He does
 there is room for nothing else.

Birth

*Do not seek the Holy
as something added on
appended to a life otherwise complete
See Moses barefoot before a burning bush
Abraham moving out at ninety and
Sarah with child…*

Part 2: In Time

"And she gave birth to her first born son and wrapped him in bands of cloth, and laid him in a manger..."

(Luke 2:7)

All births are the same
  each birth is unique
Every dappled calf
  unlike any other
The print of hand and foot
  an unduplicated miracle

How she must have wished
  to keep her child as safely
  cradled and nestled
  as in the straw that night

The passing world
  will not mark or mind
  what happens here

As she gathers the hungry mouth
  to her breast
  the ox's breath steams in the moonlight
  and somewhere
      angels sing

Brushed by the Sacred

"...and Mary said, 'let it be with me according to your word'"
(Luke 1:38)

Between the 'yes' and 'no'
  of an anonymous Bedouin girl
    there hangs in the air of that little room
  a breathless 'perhaps'
into which heaven has suspended
  its better judgment
risking the cosmic enterprise
  stars and all
as if Mary could somehow
  trump Gabriel's bid to deliver the Word and
  turn a deaf ear and
  a dead heart
  toward the divine courtship proposal

It is your 'yes'
  maid of Nazareth
  that levels the mountains
  fills the valleys and
  hands God the gift of flesh

Part 2: In Time

"And the Word became flesh and lived among us, and we have seen his glory…"

(John 1:14)

Tiny hooves pick the distance
    between Nazareth north and
    Bethlehem south
        a sixty-mile or so journey
        as jarringly real as
        the sweating swaying braying
        beast beneath her

The last contracted measure she knows
    will be as difficult…
      God's flesh delivered by human flesh…
    The Word is first a squall
     welcomed quietly by
     rough hands
     stable attendants
     a mother's whimper

Holy Spirit swells human womb with life and
    angels announce the mysterious visitation

And now all breath crystalizes
    in the desert's night air and
      Heaven's Hope
      sleeps swaddled in the straw

Brushed by the Sacred

"And she laid him in a manger because there was no room for them in the inn."

(Luke 2:7)

The house is full of pilgrims,
the innkeeper sleeps,
cushioned in profits
while golden angels populate his dreams.

In the spring he thinks
he'll add more rooms,
enclose the stable,
take on more help

Starshine flickers like flecks of fire
scampering across the bedroom wall
shepherds clatter down the alley
and silently fall afraid before the babe

The crowded city rests
swaddled in uneasy dreams
Stars wink out at the very instant
worlds are born and
wide-eyed Hope embraces
earth's new day.

Part 2: In Time

"But the angel said to the shepherds, 'Do not be afraid; for see – I am bringing you good news of great joy for all the people…'"
(Luke 2:10)

Angels forget how easily joy fills a sky,
    splits the seams of a heaven…
Angel whispers set worlds reeling,
    whirling wings tumbling galaxies
Meaning well, they shatter the crystalline darkness,
    scattering sheep and dispersing dreams
        with their commanding "Do not be afraid…"

Sorrow finds an easy berth in the smallest shelter,
    slipping into sleep and silence
Letting each world turn as it always had,
    each leaden day plodding into the next
        until all is sorrow

Angel joy yet seeks a way
    to blanket our twice-burned world
She stills her wings, quiets the gathering chorus, and
    hones shepherds' ears to hear
        a single newborn's cry

Brushed by the Sacred

"O that you would tear open the heavens and come down, so that the mountains would quake at your presence."
(Isaiah 64:1)

Christmas is manger and carols
       a baby swaddled and laid in the straw,
       shepherds, stars, sages, and angels
       peace on earth and a little quiet too.

I for one do not want the heavens torn open
       nor do I want the mountains to quake.
Isaiah's longed-for intervention –
       a world shaken like a snow globe –
       has already come.

Ask the sheep herders whose eyes were nearly blinded
       by the sight of angels tearing the air
       with the light of a thousand suns and
       filling the night with
       the wordless music of eternity.
Ask the mother whose final painful contraction birthed
       hope to a world afraid to trust it.
Ask the carpenter whose rugged hands caught the
       world's future and
       trembled at the gift of infinite possibility.

Ask the faithful of all the ages the only question to ask,
       "Has he come, is he here?"
In these not-so-silent nights find that solitary moment
       to ask and to answer with the heart.

Part 2: In Time

"In that region there were shepherds living in the fields, keeping watch over their flocks by night. Then an angel of the Lord stood before them, and the glory of the Lord shone around them, and they were terrified."
(Luke 2:8-9)

Glory always falls it seems
      to the unaware –
the wise and the watchful scan the skies
      while the loser of the draw for the midnight shift
        glances up to see the heavens explode
        raining a chorus of light on his sleeping flocks
        and his dozing companions who now
            must carry glory
          bandy-legged
              on their calloused feet and
           stammer out in rude phrasing
         what they witnessed in the sky and
            beheld in the manger straw
          that we
             in turn
                  may also tell.

Brushed by the Sacred

"The angel of the Lord appeared to Joseph in a dream and said, 'Joseph, son of David, do not be afraid to take Mary home as your wife because she has conceived what is in her by the Holy Spirit. She will give birth to a son and you must name him Jesus…'"
(Matthew 1:20-21)

Carpenters make unlikely dreamers
It is angle and grain, cut and plumb, straight and level
   that matter to woodworkers like Joseph

Carpenters know that angels do not build worlds
   only visit them
With no regard for form or precedent such messengers
   leave behind a sketchy plan that
   some worker in wood will have to flesh out
   as best anyone can
   with materials at hand

No wonder Joseph shudders now
   at the brink of dozing
   when dreams invade both sleep and she who sleeps
   making Nazareth the center of a shifting future

It is not the dream that finally frightens
   but the terrible price to embody it
Joseph knows the cost:
   gauging the dimensions of this great salvage and
   carrying the name into wakefulness…
he takes Mary home so the angel's promise can be kept.

Part 2: In Time

"People assumed that Jesus was the son of Joseph, who was the son of Heli, who was the son of Matthat, who was the son of..."
(Luke 3:24)

On a night you can't sleep
you might open your Bible to Luke 3:24 and
just start reading the family tree of a certain Joseph
      who, it was assumed,
was the father of certain Jesus of Nazareth.
If you manage to stay awake and
come to the trunk of the tree,
you will find, after wading through all the names
         (many unpronounceable), at the end:
...Enos, who was the son of Seth, who was
      the son of Adam, who was
      the son of God.

Luke went through a lot of trouble to compile
      a genealogy of a father who wasn't
           the father of a certain Jesus.
Perhaps what he meant to say was that if it were
not for Heli's son keeping faith and taking care,
the story which follows this family tree
      found in Luke's chapter three
would have never been told and
you and I would have never heard.

On a night you can't sleep,
include a certain Joseph in your prayers, and
be grateful.

Brushed by the Sacred

"…when the parents brought in the child Jesus, to do for him what was customary under the law, Simeon took him in his arms and praised God, saying, 'Master, now you are dismissing your servant in peace, according to your word; for my eyes have seen your salvation, which you have prepared in the presence of all peoples…'"

(Luke 2:27-31)

Startled, yet she surrenders the child to
   his gnarled hands
The old man peers intently through
   the glaze of aged eyes
   as the child returns his gaze
   curious and unafraid

A tiny hand is snared in Simeon's beard
The old man's dim eyes widen even more and
   his lips begin to move in a tandem dance
   a murmuring prayer giving way to a smile
   as the fingers tug the thicket of hair

To hold God's restless Peace in the manger of his arms
   to look into the eyes that witnessed the birth of stars
   to feel the touch of the hand that cradles all things –
      this is sufficient Glory for any life

He returns the child to the bewildered mother
   offers his strange, fierce blessing and
   makes his way out of the temple and into
      the light of true sight.

Part 2: In Time

"Guided by the Spirit, Simeon came into the temple; and when the parents brought in the child Jesus...he took the child in his arms and praised God...there was also a prophet, Anna...of great age who worshiped in the temple with fasting and prayer, night and day..."

(Luke 2)

They did not *happen* to be there, as if,
     accidentally,
they found themselves in the neighborhood, and stopped in...

Nor was it simply habit,
     a tip of the hat, as it were,
to a lost and distant past.
It was as if they had received an invitation
that had been somehow torn –
     the fragment bearing only the where of the
         Jerusalem Temple
but date and time long gone.

So they came faithfully, expectantly and then
     on some otherwise ordinary day
the world's future which had come out of Nazareth
    and into the arms of a peasant girl and
      her not-yet husband
         found them – old Anna and Simeon
just as the invitation had promised and
they saw, in the temple of all places,
     the face of God.

Brushed by the Sacred

Anna

She was a young woman when the workers
    began laying stone upon stone
      to build Herod's gift of temple
        to woo the Jews

She was building too, a life with
    husband, home, family
Then her husband died and with him
    her building collapsed

The temple work went on and she found herself
    in its precincts searching for the God who
      could perhaps give meaning to her loss.

Somehow amid of the clamor of construction and
    sacrifice, priestly prayers and
      workers' curses,
    she offered her gift of prayer and fasting

Until one day a peasant couple brought
    their son to be circumcised and
    their purification offering to be sacrificed and because the
widow had held on to faith
    she now beheld the face of
    the One she had awaited those many years

Herod's enticing monument had served its purpose
    and soon would be
      no more.

Part 2: In Time

Epiphany *n. A Christian festival held on January 6 in celebration of the manifestation of the divine nature of Christ to the Gentiles as represented by the Magi.*
epiphany *n. A spiritual event in which the essence of a given object of manifestation appears to the subject, as in a sudden flash of recognition.*

The Magi (from which we get the word magic)
or Wise Men (if you prefer)
or Three Kings (although we really don't know
       there were three)
follow a star (that apparently no one else noticed)
       to Bethlehem
to a certain house (not a stable)
where they found a child and his mother (Mary)
left their gifts and went home.

This tale is told to those who know no magic
aren't particularly wise
claim no royal bloodline
have never been to Bethlehem or
followed any particular star.

May this epiphany (small case, please) stir you to
look again at the people you love (and
       even those you don't)
look again at the path you have walked over the years
look again at the faces you see along the way
look again (and kindly) at your life and
remember that it is for all those faces and your own
       for the life of all
              that Mary's Child came to birth.

Brushed by the Sacred

"In the time of King Herod, after Jesus was born in Bethlehem of Judea, wise men from the East came to Jerusalem, asking, 'Where is the child who has been born king of the Jews? For we observed his star at its rising and have come to pay him homage.' When King Herod heard this, he was frightened, and all Jerusalem with him."

(Matthew 2:1-3)

The wise can sometimes be so naïve –
they stop in seedy neighborhoods to ask directions
they tip their hand
they show their cards
they follow stars

Herod, wisely, fears the child and
slyly inquires where the newborn might be found
Like every tin pot tyrant before and since,
Herod knows there is no room in
the kingdom for two kings

Out of his world of shadows and whispers,
blood and fears,
Herod sees no other way and
launches the troops
Bethlehem feels his shock and awe,
but the child springs free
from the king's deathtrap.

Part 2: In Time

"Where is the child who has been born king of the Jews? We have seen his star at its rising, and have come to pay him homage."
(Matthew 2:2)

Draw a line from Babylon to Jerusalem
Assume the Magi traveled straight as the crow flies
   toward a star winking in the west

Take that line and lay it over our troubled map
   and you intersect Iran, Iraq, Jordan, Saudi Arabia and
   Israel

The sands have shifted long ago, of course, and
   new faiths have been forged from desert fire

Now each king follows his own reckoning and
   every mother's child makes his way
   under a starless sky

And even if that same star should rise again
   the ancient route is strewn with barbed barriers and
   choked by a diplomacy tangled beyond
   the unraveling of the wisest

But if you are bearing gifts and would
   make that journey

You need not follow those same coordinates
But simply gather up what is of greatest value to you
Find the place where it is most needed and
   give it away

Brushed by the Sacred

The faces of those who walk that journey
   become almost like stars themselves
   leading the way for the rest
   to that place where Life has come to die and
      rise again
           for us all.

Part 2: In Time

"When Herod saw that he had been tricked by the wise men, he was infuriated, and he sent and killed all the children in and around Bethlehem who were two years old or under, according to the time that he had learned from the wise men."

(Matthew 2:16)

The wise men, unwisely, disrupt Bethlehem's peace
   pointing Herod to the star-crossed spot
   where a mother holds her unlike-no-other child

Now the mothers weep in Bethlehem's streets and
   three refugees slip by night
   south across the border

Tyrants opt for the same tired path in every age,
   flailing sword against the wind
   while Hope still whistles through the steel

Love must again take to flight and
   find a refuge in the unknown Nazareth
   of the heart

Until, journeying south once more,
   must break both a mother's heavy heart and
   a tomb's cold door.

Brushed by the Sacred

"As for Mary, she treasured all these things and pondered them in her heart."

(Luke 2:19)

There is room enough
  in the casket of the heart
      to carry a lifetime's occasions of
          ruby sunrise
          diamond glint on emerald sea
          nets like abandoned necklaces
              pearled with brine
          water to wine and to water again
              for the cleansing of topaz feet

There is room enough, but barely,
  in the casket of the heart
      for her child's future cascading into her present
          angels' wings fluttering
              the Magi muttering
          to tell the ageless Somehow that
              heaven has engaged earth and
          Word will yet marry flesh

Wherever there is room enough
  in the receptive womb of any willing heart.

Part 2: In Time

Once in a while
        in all of the not-so-silent nights since
                the dream returns and
we wake
        remembering
the incense of straw and
the vibration of air whirring
        with word and wings and
        a song unheard and
        never forgotten

We surface to the day
        strangely born
                again

Brushed by the Sacred

Now we stand at the edge of an age
    monitoring the odometer of the years
    preparing to turn
        dating checks and letters
        by a distant Birth
            a receding star that somehow
            maps our journey yet
Do not write this age's story
    by the dim lamps of memory
    locking Hope in the constraining calendar
but rather
    by the light ahead
    tracing a way through the unlikely holiness of
        stable and
    the predictable meagerness of
        tomb's swaddling bands
        to the promise remembered and
        yet to be kept by the
            One who begins and ends
            every age
        and shelters us amid the uncertain winter
            of our turning time.

Death

See Isaiah as the temple pillars shake
a hot coal sizzling on his lips
Noah bobbing in the storm
Jonah in the whale's belly
See Paul flattened on the Damascus road
Lazarus shuffling toward the light
See Jesus on a government-issue cross...

Part 2: In Time

"When the people saw that Moses delayed to come down from the mountain, the people gathered around Aaron and said to him, 'Come make gods for us, who shall go before us; as for this Moses, the man who brought us out of Egypt, we do not know what has become of him.'"

(Exodus 32:1)

Out of sight, out of mind:
   How long does it take for a people to forget that they
   were once slaves in another life?

What have you done for us lately, Moses?
Red Sea parting, manna in the morning, quail at night,
   water from the rock, not to mention the ten plagues
   that finally loosened Pharaoh's grip, and, oh yes,
   the cloud by day and fire by night –
       that was all so yesterday

This invisible God you are always talking to
   is only occasionally available and therefore
   we have a short list of things we need and
   since you don't seem to be coming back,
   we'll ask your brother:
        - a good reliable GPS to get us out of this desert
        - some Styrofoam containers to keep
          the leftover manna and quail
        - air conditioning, Wi-Fi, bottled water
        - weekends off and reliable childcare
And if we come up with anything of a
   more spiritual nature,
       not religious,
we're sure Aaron will come through for us –
   he doesn't go near the mountain.

Brushed by the Sacred

"Six days later, Jesus took with him Peter and James and John and led them up a high mountain where they could be alone by themselves. There in their presence he was transfigured: his clothes became dazzling white…"

(Mark 9:2-3)

One morning at age ninety-five
she looked in the mirror
  and asked, "Who is that old lady?" –
    a question that does not require being led
      up a high mountain.

A glance in the mirror is occasion enough
  to prompt the question,
    "Who is that?"

Sometimes a face you thought you knew,
  lived with,
    grew up with,
  called wife, husband, brother, sister, mother, father,
    friend
      suddenly flares up fresh and new.

We tag it transfiguration, this Jesus dazzling white,
  seen by but a timid trio
A hunch would hazard a guess that, for a moment,
  they saw him as he really was and
    for the rest of their lives
      never quite the same
        the image burned.

We were not there, you and I, nor did we see,
  but out of the corner of my eye,

Part 2: In Time

like a firefly on a summer night,
        I catch a glimpse in a face I know well and
              discover myself
                      transfigured.

Brushed by the Sacred

"Ashes to ashes, dust to dust…"
was once another way to say
"Nothing lasts" and
"Nothing stays the same…"

The preacher brushes the dirt from experienced hands,
the funeral director knowingly nods,
the procession somberly scatters from the graveside…

We return to life left off, looking for what lasts, grieving what
has been lost:
the Nothing that never stays the same.
Ashes slashed across a forehead are no metaphor
for those who stand at the volcano's rim or
ground zero on a cloudless day

Wednesday's ashes can come on any day
to mark us mortal and fashioned of dust
Until the day we are remembered by
the one who formed us
who sends the Wind to gather what has been scattered
and on the first day of the week that has but one day…
brushes the ashes from our foreheads and
breathes us to life without end.

Part 2: In Time

Ash Wednesday (again)

There is more forehead this year than last
to offer as a sort of canvas upon which
another hand may trace the blackened cross

I will wear it out into the night where
some stranger will wonder, perhaps,
the meaning of the mark…
the stranger being too polite to ask and
I too timid to explain,
even if I could

The custom, I fear, is fading in a world
that recoils from such blatancy
preferring lame excuse over
costly grace

Nor am I inspired by the televised celebrity confession
instantly received by
an audience all too eager to forgive
wrongs they never felt

But long after the ashes have disintegrated
I will remember the touch of a neighbor's hand upon my brow
confirming, without words,
that we may walk another year together,
God willing, and
that our sin, while real,
shall not keep us from our journey's end.

Brushed by the Sacred

"Create in me a clean heart, O God, and put a new and right spirit within me."

(Psalm 51:10)

In need of a transplant…
    a clean heart, a right spirit…

I approach the season wondering
    if perhaps the old pump may have
    a few more miles in it
        if I don't ask too much of it.

Transplants can be tricky…
    finding a Donor who's also a match…
        the surgery…
            the recovery… and, of course,
                the possibility of rejection.

What, I wonder, are the long-term effects
    on the rest of the body?
    Memory loss?
    Personality changes?

But what choice does a person have
    with ashes splashed on the forehead and
    spring on the way?

Part 2: In Time

Ashes and Mud

Spring is coming, but it is not here… and no one
   trusts the warming air… we've been fooled before

Hope looks over her shoulder, keeps fingers crossed
   there will still be ice and
   someone should whisper to the buds,
   "Not yet…"

The mud freezes and thaws,
   yesterday's tracks memorialized in today's cold
   becoming hollows to hold the rain
Winter withdraws her white robe and leaves a gritty
   remnant of discarded dreams that sadly
   sparkle like the silver icicles fallen
   from a tree abandoned at the curb

It is the uncertain season…
   the season of ashes and mud…
   we feel the breeze from a distant garden where
   three women met a familiar stranger
   in the chilly dawn and
somehow we must make our way there too
   with mud on our shoes and ashes on our faces
with the old taste of our own fear and dying
   in our mouths but a strange new pounding in the
   heart propelling us to that vacated room from which
   life spills its light into a breathless world and the
   uncertain season slips finally into an eternal spring

Brushed by the Sacred

"Jesus, full of the Holy Spirit, returned from the Jordan and was led by the Spirit in the wilderness, where for forty days he was tempted by the devil. He ate nothing at all during those days, and when they were over, he was famished."

(Luke 4:1-2)

It would not take me forty days to find my appetite
        I do not need a desert to make me thirst
Quickly driven to deprivation, I fold my tent
        at the most distant threat
Once or twice lured by heroism, I endured
        until the temptation passed

I would abstain this season…
        …from making promises I cannot keep
        …from hoping too much and trusting too deeply

The devil is worrisome, of course,
        so I am wary of fresh bread and too high places

But it is the Galilean who troubles me more:
        I fear that in an unguarded moment
                he may snare me with a word
        until I am hopelessly entangled in his net of love
                and dragged thrashing onto the shores
        of a strangely distant yet near kingdom
                into which I will be lured for good

Part 2: In Time

Go to the Devil

"Jesus, full of the Holy Spirit, returned from the Jordan and was led by the Spirit in the wilderness, where for forty days he was tempted by the devil."

(Luke 4:1)

Still wet from John's washing,
   the sound of wings at his back,
   he enters the season of mirage and illusion
   in which stones are bread and wind whistles what
   dare not be

Devil's playground of possibilities: a world redeemed
   by strutting power (a magician's wand of every age)
   fitting by force the wedge of good intentions
   into the notch of humanity's need

The Tempter's scenario is eminently sensible:
   the policy is sound, there is expert consensus,
   coalitions can be built around it,
   collateral damage will be minimal

The Son of Man stands alone between
   Satan's argument and
  the land beyond the Jordan where
   the struggle between logic and Mystery
   must finally cross

On Satan's turf he stakes his "No" three times,
   marking the limit of his first attack,
   the final assault to come later,
   not in the desert, but a garden

There, while disciples sleep,
    the Son of Man plants his "Yes" three times
    and by his dying, gives rise to life.

Part 2: In Time

"The Passover of the Jews was near, and Jesus went up to Jerusalem. In the temple he found people selling cattle, sheep, and doves, and the money-changers seated at their tables. Making a whip of cords, he drove all of them out of the temple, both the sheep and the cattle. He also poured out the coins of the money-changers and overturned their tables. He told those who were selling the doves, 'Take these things out of here! Stop making my Father's house a market-place!' His disciples remembered that it was written, 'Zeal for your house will consume me.'"

(John 2:13-17)

Who *is* this turner of tables with whip of cords
   who strides into the seat of legitimate commerce and
   scatters livestock, brokers, and earnings reports
   out the door of what he calls his "Father's house"?

What happened to the gentle Jesus, meek and mild,
   who gathered children in tender blessing,
   told stories of seeds and lost sheep,
   runaway boys and wounded travelers?

When I hear again of his coming and consider in this season of disparities – the rich more noted,
   the poor forgotten, the middle disappearing –
   will he turn a blind eye to our constant scheming?

"Come, Lord Jesus!" we blithely pray,
   but should he, and he surely will,
   at which table will he find me sitting, and
   will I tremble at his coming?

Brushed by the Sacred

"And the inscription of the charge against him read, 'The king of the Jews.' And with him they crucified two thieves, one on his right and one on his left."

(Matthew 27:37-38)

It takes a thief, they say,
        to catch a thief.
Stealing the blindness from the beggar's eyes
   picking Caesar's coin from the Pharisees' pocket
   snatching Lazarus from his crypt
   this highborn felon who would
   pad paradise with stolen goods:
        no coin too tarnished,
        no specimen too shabby
           to store with all the rest.

Beside the fishing nets,
   the tax collector's purse, and
   my threadbare dreams
   he takes my heart, as well
        hardened item of no account
   now strangely treasured and
           alive at last

This third and greatest thief
   has unlocked heaven's gate and
        tossed away the key.

Part 2: In Time

"Then one of the twelve, who was called Judas Iscariot, went to the chief priests and said, 'What will you give me if I betray him to you?' They paid him thirty pieces of silver. And from that moment he began to look for an opportunity."
(Matthew 26:14-16)

Every life arcs to a single moment
  after which nothing can much add or take away:
      Pilate washing his hands
      the rich young ruler walking away
      the blessed one burying the entrusted talent
      Judas picking up the chief priests' purse
         the sound of closing doors

But what of Peter's triple denial?
      Thomas' trust of touch alone?
      James and John craving thrones for the asking?
      the rest who waited for grave-visiting women
         to sound the "all clear"?

The margin of salvation seems so razor-thin:
      a brave word bravely spoken
      a solitary "yes"
      a purse refused
         ...but wait...

Every life bows to a single moment
  after which nothing can much add or take away
      unless it be discovered buried in
        that garden tomb where Hope was laid but
would not rest until every life and every moment
      be handed over, ransomed and made forever
          new.

Brushed by the Sacred

He came to Simon Peter, who said to him, 'Lord, are you going to wash my feet?' Jesus answered, 'You do not know now what I am doing, but later you will understand.' Peter said to him, 'You will never wash my feet.' Jesus answered, 'Unless I wash you, you have no share with me.' After he had washed their feet, had put on his robe, and had returned to the table, he said to them, 'Do you know what I have done to you? You call me Teacher and Lord – and you are right, for that is what I am. So if I, your Lord and Teacher, have washed your feet, you also ought to wash one another's feet. For I have set you an example, that you also should do as I have done to you.'"

(John 13)

Gnarled and bunioned, blistered, splayed and dirty…
    Lord, leave them to ache and itch;
They are beneath you.

Anoint my head with oil, overflow my cup,
    cleanse me from sin (pleasant metaphor!),
but leave my feet alone.

Your kneeling is unbecoming,
    your touch too much to bear;
paralyzed, I fear that I will shatter.

Darkness beckons, wine no longer warms,
    bread is broken, scattered, and now with
leaden, unfeeling feet we shuffle to prayers and sleep.

I suspect where this is leading
    as I lay my head upon a stone and
hear the tread of the countless faithful…

Part 2: In Time

I, Simon, will belt my waist with borrowed towel and
      recalling my Master's words in my heart and
my Lord's hands upon my instep
      will bend to find my place at the throne of God.

First Coming

"He came into the world – the world he had created – and the world failed to recognize him."

(John 1:10) [Phillips]

It was not the best time to step in…
    what with all the bickering and infighting,
    the unresponsive bureaucracy,
    the religious crazies, the lousy economy, and
    the poor poorer by the day…

To just show up that way with only
    one advance man
    wearing animal skins and
    sporting locust wings in his beard…
  to appear and then disappear into the desert…
  only to reappear,
    gather a few followers,
    irritate the authorities,
    overturn some tables,
    be arrested for sedition,
    die between two thieves, and…

Now we are left with a handful of stories,
    a few hard-to-corroborate reports, and
    the overpowering suspicion
    (praise God!)
        that we are not alone.

Part 2: In Time

"Then God said to the man, 'You may eat indeed of all the trees in the garden. Nevertheless of the tree of the knowledge of good and evil you are not to eat for on the day you eat of it you shall most surely die.'"
(Genesis 2:16-17)

But he didn't die, not in the moment
he tasted the forbidden fruit.
He blamed her, she blamed the snake,
but who are we to blame any of them?

They don't die: the apple… or whatever it was…
isn't poisoned (that's a fairy tale),
no lightning strikes (that's Hollywood),
the sky doesn't fall (that's a children's story).

But now they know.
There is a shadow where once there was only shade,
a voice once familiar is now strange,
they look at each other across a distance
that was not there before.

What do they know?
       the garden is not theirs
       nothing remains the same
       there will be a last time

Yet there is another garden where
in anguished tears
the truth of the first loss was faced
by One who would die the first man's death.

Brushed by the Sacred

And still another garden where
        Hope could not be laid to rest, and
        an eager Peace gathers all things
                to the Gardener's heart.

Part 2: In Time

"Then he took it down, wrapped it in a linen cloth, and laid it in a rock-hewn tomb where no one had ever been laid." (Luke 23:53)

Already the body stiffens in the constricting linen,
   the miracle of birth undone
   by the miracle of unbecoming:
       the sudden loss of name and breath.

The freefall from the Father is finished
   on the bedrock of Joseph's virgin tomb where
   the Arimathean thought he'd reside beside
       the deceased at his own last.

The price of flesh is paid, the entry fee for
   joining the anonymous hosts who went ahead and
   the Son of God becomes an unwieldy husk
       at the mercy of strangers.

This second swaddling at the hands of a second Joseph
   ties off the cord of what might have been,
   once, and now
       for all?

But there are always those who,
   having seen two miracles, wait for a third and
   come to the garden tombs bearing spices in one hand
       and hope in the other.

Resurrection

See the empty tomb…

Part 2: In Time

"But Peter got up and ran to the tomb; stooping and looking in, he saw the linen cloths by themselves; then he went home, amazed at what had happened."

(Luke 24:12)

Where do you go from there
  but home?
To the familiar, the known, and
   everything is how you remembered it,
   everything is where you left it.

The breakfast dishes wait in the sink,
  the bed lies unmade,
   the coffee cup stands half-filled and cold,
  the paper rests unread.

Every thing is where you left it, and
  not one thing is the same

There is no more peculiar house than
  the one you return to from the cemetery

There is no stranger world than
  the one you enter
  having been to the empty tomb

Brushed by the Sacred

"There will be no more death, and no more mourning or sadness. The world of the past has gone."
                                            (Revelation 21:4)

All that is buried, is not raised
he leaves behind the linen wrappings and
more besides

The women were the first to hear,
then John and Simon Peter,
finally, the rest which, I suppose,
includes you, me, and those to come

Now King Death wanders, homeless,
still pretending,
Pretender to a kingdom that has been
sacked and dismantled

If you see him, when you see him,
point him to that garden tomb,
invite him to check out the floor plan and then
make his bed there

Let him rule that little space and
wait away the hours
until the gardener returns to
roll the stone door back into place
Let him wrap himself in the lifeless linens and
mourn forever all that he has lost.

Part 2: In Time

"You are looking for Jesus of Nazareth who was crucified. He has been raised' he is not here."

(Mark 16:6)

If they had found what they were looking for –
   all would have been lost:
  that's the truth and the terror of it.
No wonder they ran wordless
   from the spot
fearful
as the absence
       filled every place with the possibility that
           at any moment
      there he might be
                  or not
Now the myrrh remains unspent and
  the gravestone ineffective;
 the women run and
 the Word
      still to be spoken
            runs before.

Brushed by the Sacred

"So they went out and fled from the tomb, for terror and amazement had seized them; and they said nothing to anyone, for they were afraid."

(Mark 16:8)

In the face of all the deaths this dying century
   has witnessed and forgotten,
all the unmarked graves that inhale
   breath and dream alike:
there is little left to terrify us and
   less to amaze.

So we decorate our Easters with idle chatter
   against the silence of buried hope and
prop up a guard lest life break out and
   shake our shallow sleep.

Come, Holy Terror, and shatter the darkness of
   night's grey grip and scatter us running to
   the dawn and beyond
to the waiting ones who have heard
      but not seen.

Brand our faces with the impress of that stone –
   an etching of the splintering light that
      cracks opens every grave and
blind our hearers for a while
   so that they must read our lips
      with the braille of faith and
        with us
        believe.

Part 2: In Time

"After the Sabbath, and towards dawn on the first day of the week, Mary of Magdala and the other Mary went to visit the sepulcher."
(Matthew 28:1)

Who was that "other" Mary who
  also visited the tomb that first Easter?
Why are there no St. Other Mary churches or
  hospitals or colleges?
Why are no prayers offered to her,
  no feast days held in her honor?

Here's a proposal:
  to elevate her as the patron saint of
    those who fasten their names to the underside of
    a casserole dish offered for a funeral luncheon and
    those who place their names carefully on the
    sympathy card and
    those who sign their names legibly on the list to
    deliver flowers as well as wash the dishes and
    clean up the kitchen.

The Other Mary saw that the stone was moved
  out of the way and
she trusts that she will meet him again
  among those he calls her to serve.

She will know him when she sees him and
  he will call her too
      by name.

Brushed by the Sacred

"Why do you look for the living among the dead? He is not here, but has risen. Remember how he told you, while he was still in Galilee, that the Son of Man must be handed over to sinners, and be crucified, and on the third day rise again."

(Luke 24:5-6)

In that dead stick prose
   that angels seem to favor
   the two dazzling men remind the women
       that this is not new news,
       that he covered this in Galilee
as if to suggest that they should check their notes
   to find the reference
   filed under… what?
       Third day?
       Rise again?

Angels are trained in plain delivery…
   light on the special effects…
   leaving the trumpets at home:
even though they were the first
   to find the grave empty
   they determined that
       it was for the women principally
       to feel the void of his absence

Then, anticipating, fearing that they bolt and run and
   begin to doubt what they did not see
the news-bearers had them trace the homely lessons
   he once taught them so
   they could, and would,
   in the first brave scrawl of faith writ simple,
   remind the others, deaf with fears,

Part 2: In Time

        of what he once said into their thick ears
They did so, of course,
  as a mother reassures an ailing child,
  until with the dawn the fever breaks, and
  Simon hurries to find
      what he already knows
           is true.

Preemptive Strike

"And he will destroy on this mountain the shroud that is cast over all peoples, the sheet that is spread over all nations; he will swallow up death forever."

(Isaiah 25:7)

The shroud is cast, the sheet is spread
  hiding beneath it
  all the terror justified by lengthy speeches,
  well-reasoned arguments
  invoking honor to Allah, to Jehovah,
      from a thousand throats
        each one silenced in its day and
        taken up in the amnesia of each generation

Who dares to raise this pall?
Who dares take on this horror and
      lay it down again?

Tombward all are bound,
  the dying bearing the dead,
  who will deal with the stone,
  who will roll it back?

Who can believe what is reported?
The alabaster jar shatters at the women's feet
  for deep within that earthen pocket
  the graveclothes lie folded while
      Life unencumbered
      strides forth to lift the veil.

Part 2: In Time

"Then Simon Peter came, following him, and went into the tomb. He saw the linen wrappings lying there, and the cloth that had been on Jesus' head, not lying with the linen wrappings but rolled up in a place by itself. Then the other disciple, who reached the tomb first, also went in, and he saw and believed; for as yet they did not understand the scripture, that he must rise from the dead. Then the disciples returned to their homes."

(John 20:6-10)

The words fall like stones in a pool...
   the inventory of an unmade room
   abandoned in the night

Useless clues hinting of a palpable presence
   that keeps the very air yet charged...
   linen wrappings shucked like husk,
   head cloth casually peeled and tossed

They see and believe... but what?
   that the women spoke the truth?
   that the stone was moved?
       the body missing?

Seeing is not always believing...
   seeing is simply seeing.

Believing begins when the words tumble out and
   the long, breathless telling recounts just this:
       we ran to the tomb and
       found it empty, and
       found it empty,
           and found...

Brushed by the Sacred

"And suddenly there was a great earthquake; for an angel of the Lord, descending from heaven, came and rolled back the stone and sat on it. His appearance was like lightning, and his clothing white as snow. For fear of him the guards shook and became like dead men."
(Matthew 28:2-4)

There comes a time when heaven,
        tired of coaxing and
        weary of metaphors,
splits the difference between earth and sky
        with fire and terror
        to direct, if for a moment, our attention
        toward possibilities we had not entertained:
- that cemeteries cannot hold their own when angels come down to play
- that even a watched grave spills over
- that real life, if we were to encounter it, would freeze us in our tracks
- that lightning, earthquake, and snow…
    even all at once…
  are not much of anything compared to
      what comes next

There comes a time when heaven,
        tired of coaxing and
        weary of metaphors,
peels back the veil of sky and
                reveals the face of God.

Part 2: In Time

"Then he showed them his hands and side, and when the disciples saw the Lord they were overjoyed."

(John 20:20)

So the heaven-sent Son carries back to the Father
   his cross-cut hands, never forgotten, ever forgiven

But with them, perhaps, he also carries
   the taste of new wine and salt tears,
   the sound of laughing children and chirping birds,
   the smell of fresh bread and spring rain,
   the touch of a dear friend's hand,
   the sight of a stranger's smile.

And the Father, having birthed his Child
   from the grave
   inventories all that the prodigal has
   brought with him, and
   with a word that heaven has long awaited,
   breathes upon his world once more and
       calls it
            good.

Brushed by the Sacred

There are any number of tour guides in Palestine
   who will cheerfully point out
   the place where they buried
   a certain Jesus.

It is of little consequence that
   there is some disagreement among scholars and
   keepers of cemetery records
   as to which particular grave was
        precisely his.

No matter,
   you need not travel such a distance to see
   that he has bought out Death's interest
   in all such real estate and
   has remodeled them into reception rooms
        for his Kingdom.

Graciously now, there are no anonymous tombs
   for each one has been imprinted with the sign of
   his glorious, stubborn
   unwillingness to let stone or sod or human hate
        have the last word.

This is a piece of good news
   that you probably won't hear on
   any gravestone tour of Death's crumbled bailiwick.

Better yet:
   the only sorrow left to feel is for
   the ousted King Death for
        he has no place to call home.

Part 2: In Time

"Just after daybreak, Jesus stood on the beach; but the disciples did not know that it was Jesus. Jesus said to them, 'Children, you have no fish, have you?' They answered him, 'No.' He said to them, 'Cast the net to the right side of the boat, and you will find some.' So they cast it, and now they were not able to haul it in because there were so many fish."
(John 20:4-6)

It is the day after Easter and what has changed?
The same nets hang where they were suspended
   three years before,
the boats rock gently in the shallows,
   sails wrapped tightly beneath the yardarms
but fishermen are optimists by nature:
   today will be different
   today there will be fish

All through the night,
   they cast and
   recast their nets until
hands blistered and bleeding
Empty, their boats ride high in the water
   until, at last, leaden arms heaved the oars
   shoreward

It is only then that the carpenter called the question
   to which he already knew the answer
It is the catch of a lifetime as well as the last
What do carpenter-rabbis know of fishing?

Enough, it would seem,
   to know where the fish hide
   and to net the people who seek them

Rebirth

*Do not seek the Holy
The Holy will find you
And when He does
there is room for nothing else.*

Part 2: In Time

"Jesus said to Mary, do not hold on to me, for I have not yet ascended..."

(John 20:17a)

The touch of cloth and flesh
  taste of tears
    the reassuring rock-
      dense and real-
        sweet smell of April
  sun melting the morning
      fears fading with a name spoken
        in love's familiar voice

From the deep lake of all our yesterdays,
  out of the river of memory
    dammed by the tomb's cold stone,
      comes the throbbing pulse of recognition

This is what we cling to and
  to which he will not let us hold until,
    arising from our sight,
      he hallows all our time
      turning it to living waters
        to bloom the desert of our desires
and promising,
  once ascended,
      to return

Ascension

"While he was blessing them, he withdrew from them and was carried up into heaven."
(Luke 24:51)

We would have held him
   clung to what we knew in flesh
      our flesh and his

The scars real and reassuring,
  never healed,
  open as a plundered grave,
  glowing, raw and flaming

Full forty days he lingered with us,
  never tiring,
  as if day and night were all the same to him
  telling us what we knew
      but did not know

Then he was gone and never gone and
  we were alone and never alone
  while the peace he gave us
      gave us no peace

Back we ran in fearful joy to Jerusalem,
  to Egypt, to Greece, to Spain and
  the distant Isles, and yes,
  of course,
      to Rome

Part 2: In Time

To plant the seed he told us must die
   if there is to be a harvest and
   rise again in the
       breaking of bread

"When the day of Pentecost had come, they were all together in one place."

(Acts 2:1)

Perhaps it would help,
  before we draw up any more rules,
  adopt any more policies,
  bless any more crusades (moral or martial),
  launch any more offensives…
      to simply be together
         in one place

It would do us good
  to listen to the beating of our hearts
  to ponder the pulsing of hands held and
  to feel the breath of forgiveness
      on our cheeks

Let the Wind speak for itself, so that
  spirits exhaling like sails in its wake
  may carry life
      to a waiting world.

Part 2: In Time

Pentecost: **As Improv**

"All of them were filled with the Holy Spirit and began to speak in other languages, as the Spirit gave them ability."
(Acts 2:4)

suppose the copier broke down and
  there were no bulletins?
the preacher's sermon went missing?
the organist overslept? and
the lights failed to come on?
would we still have church?
would we still be church
  off the cuff,
    a capella,
      without notes or prompts?
would someone say a word of hope,
  someone start a song,
    someone dare a prayer,
      someone light a candle?
can Mystery still intrude,
can Spirit still surprise?
there are days I wish the Wind
  would sweep away bulletins, reports, hymnals,
    sheet music, sermon notes
blowing through the pipes some new song
  everyone would sing
    rattling windows and knocking doors off the hinges
  taking our breath away and giving us new breath…
and there are days I fear It might

Brushed by the Sacred

"When the day of Pentecost had come, they were all together in one place. And suddenly from heaven they heard what sounded like the rush of a violent wind, and it filled the entire house where they were sitting. And something appeared to them that seemed like tongues of fire..."

(Acts 2:1-2)

Sounded like...
  seemed like...

We hunger for sharper certainty:
  who were *they*? and
  where was this place? and
  was it wind or not?
Tongues of fire?!

Had we been there the picture would be clearer,
  the evidence more believable, and
  the report more precise.

So tell me...

  what is it like to fall in love? and
  what did you feel when you
      - first glimpsed the ocean
      - learned to ride a two-wheeler
      - cashed your first paycheck
      - held your firstborn?
what brings tears to your eyes and
what makes you laugh and why?
what does fresh bread smell like and
what day would you live over if you could?

Part 2: In Time

You cannot catch the wind in a net of facts…
  it takes a sail stitched in imagery,
  a kite that dances on heaven's sighs
      held by a tether of words and wonder.

Brushed by the Sacred

"The hand of the Lord came upon me, and he brought me out by the spirit of the Lord and set me down in the middle of a valley; it was full of bones. He led me all round them; there were very many lying in the valley, and they were very dry. He said to me, 'Mortal, can these bones live?' I answered, 'O Lord God, you know.'"

(Ezekiel 37:1-3)

The landscape of our age is littered
with the bones of dreams deferred and
hope hollowed by gnawing doubt
as we settle for the little peace
of momentary quiet and
hear the empty promise
that we can always be both safe and free
Can these bones live?

Can dreams be rejoined when sleep and
hearts are broken?

Can hope rend the shroud of disbelief?
We have heard your answer, Lord God,
in the rolled-back gravestone of an Easter morn,
echoed in the wind that whistles away the dust
of settled accommodation to business-as-usual, and
in the fire that consumes the dross of compromising
collaboration with death's whispered lie.

Breathe us to life, and
these bones shall indeed live.

Part 2: In Time

"I prophesied as he commanded me, and breath came into them, and they lived, and stood on their feet, a vast multitude."
(Ezekiel 37:10)
"And suddenly from heaven there came a sound like the rush of a violent wind, and it filled the entire house where they were sitting."
(Acts 2:2)

Choked with mucous, wet from the womb,
   the newborn lungs bellow out for first catch of air
and launch in a single breath
   the arc of a lifetime's respiring

Willing captive to needing flesh, the rushing wind
   bends to nurture the blood that bathes
every far-flung cell with vermilion grace
   offering life in generous reflexive measure

Then exhaled to serve again as shout of warning,
   word of hope or praise, whisper of affection, or,
even more extravagantly, to whistle home
   the sheep from forage and the prodigal from exile

Unwilling to conspire with dividing walls,
   the rushing wind will not abide the icy seclusion
of a people perpetually awaiting the end
   of the heart's long winter

But moves, with keening interest, to the rustling center
   of a church dry-boned but not forgotten
ready, at last, to rise
   hot and holy to its feet.

Simon Peter at Pentecost

"And there appeared to them tongues as of fire; these separated and came to rest on the head of each of them."
(Acts 2:3)

Now the familiar fire returns
   burning like a madness.
I hear the voices mixed and strange and
   yet I understand.
In them the Voice that called me out
   from nets and brine and sail and
brought me with Andrew, James, John, and
   all the rest to this windowed room.

The irresistible dancing fire
   calling us in the name of love away from
all we thought we loved
   to tell a strange story in a land of mixed peoples.
I have discovered my voice at last and
   there will be no more denials
but only the leading dancing fire
   lighting the way to the Light and
       home.

Part 2: In Time

"So then, my brothers and sisters, when you come together to eat, wait for one another."

(I Corinthians 11:33)

This is not fast food. It will wait.
This table has been set for near twenty centuries and will be set yet again.
*"With Angels and Archangels and
    all the company of heaven..."*
so the old prayer reminds, inviting us
to take our place at table.

The house is ablaze with light,
the door is open,
the smell of fresh bread, still warm,
    wafts into the street,
the wine glistens in every glass...
"Come as you are..."
the invitation is clear and familiar:
    This is yours.

Labor Day... a prayer

Lord Jesus, one day
you shook the sawdust from your hair and
   left to take up other work.

Did the blind man feel the callouses
   when you touched his eyelids?

Did Simon Peter, slipping beneath the waves,
   feel the strength of your arms
   as you pulled him to safety?

You knew splinters and sweat,
   you have felt the weight of heavy beam.

Be with those whose labor and worth
   is measured in pieces and pounds;
who must wrestle with fire and storm;
who cross lonely miles while others sleep;
who clean and carry what we leave behind;
whose work goes unnoticed unless undone;
who tend to those so often forgotten.

May we find ourselves at your side,
   working for a world
   where wages are fair and all labor is respected.

Then, when our work is done,
may we hear you say,
      "Well done, good and faithful servant,
       enter into your Master's joy."

Epilogue

Epilogue

Beginning

                In the beginning was the word…
and all the Creator had to do was say it and
      it was so.
"Be!" – a single verb uttered, and
      a thousand billion worlds melded into existence
The Son named each one
      rejoicing in the Father's handiwork
           while the Spirit fussed over it all
      breathing life into every corner
Then the Son spied a blue marble world
      nestled in a bird's nest of galaxy and
           held it in his hand
The Father,
      charmed by the Son's admiration,
           asked him what he would call it
and the Son,
      gazing at its swirling clouds and
           white-capped oceans,
                  said:
              "I think I'll call it
                home."